KNOW WHO THE F*CK YOU ARE

RAW & UNFILTERED TRANSMISSIONS TO HELP US ALL REMEMBER WHO WE REALLY ARE

DR. BRETT JONES

CONTENTS

AUTHOR BIO

A visionary, an entrepreneur, a shaman, a father, a husband, and humble servant of the divine principles of life, Dr. Brett Jones is undoubtedly a rare and unique expression of a human. His artistry takes many forms from working hands on with people through chiropractic adjustments, speaking and teaching internationally, creating online programs that span the globe, educating through workshops and social media, to connecting with his local community.

After the tragic and sudden death of his brother at a young age, an event that forever changed the trajectory of his life, he spent years searching outside of self for connection. Struggle, grit, and hardwork propelled him into a collegiate football career in which Dr. Brett witnessed first hand the destructive path of prescription drug abuse and the limitations of the medical model. Looking for an alternative, chiropractic found him. The philosophy of chiropractic, is what set the stage for a life commitment to mastery of self, his craft, and raising the consciousness of humanity.

Through his constant pursuit of growth he is no stranger to overcoming the perceived limitations of the mind and body, and facilitating those same kinds of deep transformational experiences for others. A few projects he has had his hand in creating are:

The Source Chiropractic - a family empowerment chiropractic office representing unity and diversity *(www.thesourcechiropractic.com)*

Kairos Training Culture - a global collaborative community dedicated to evolving the art of chiropractic *(www.kairostrainingculture.com)*

Kairos Presents - a seminar company sourced in self-development, spiritual awakening, and radical support with a tribe mentality *(www.kairospresents.com)*

The Healing Immersion Experience - a chiropractic immersive experience to facilitate healing for those whose conditions are not improving with typical chiropractic or allopathic care *(www.healingimmersionexperience.com)*

Sacred Masculine Podcast- a podcast built for inclusivity of all genders to walk a path in embracing their power in reverence for both feminine and masculine energies *(www.sacredmasculine.com)*

META Moon Challenge - Lunar based challenges for SELF-discovery, accountability, and empowerment *(www.metamoonchallenge.com)*

Dr. Brett's cultivation of self and ability to curate experiences continues to serve and also transcend the chiropractic profession. This book is the first of many offerings that will continue to bridge the gap between health care professionals, thought leaders, entrepreneurs, scientists, and the general public.

FOREWORD

According to the Achuar warrior tribe of the Amazonian basin, there are three different types of leaders that people look to in times of need.

The War Chief is responsible for keeping the community safe during times of struggle, danger or famine. They are sought to lead when the tribe is facing its fears.

The Peace Chief is the bearer of generosity and abundance in times of tribal growth. They are chosen to lead when life is plentiful.

And then there's the Shaman. The Shaman is the guide and healer who transcends time. Wise and strong, he is the keeper of keys and doors. He shows us the world as it is and helps us understand the journey of life.

Humans need all three leaders working in harmony to survive.

But the Shaman's voice has been drowned out in recent years—muffled under the cacophony of a technological explosion that's still happening. Our way of being is becoming distorted by the breakneck pace of our own evolution.

The role of guide has been vacant for centuries and we've been left in waiting.

It seems as though in our race to connect, the world has left billions of people feeling more disconnected from Source than ever before.

Many are looking for answers in the form of a belief system, political movement or social group. Bogged down by the haze and confusion of media, politics, and dogma, we are running scared in circles, waiting and wishing for somebody to show us the way. Hoping somebody will tell us about our purpose and ourselves.

But the Shaman isn't coming to save us. We must look inside.

In order to fulfill your highest potential in this lifetime, you will have to undergo your own journey of personal mastery, evolution and healing.

It's time for you to wake up and become your own guide.

Know Who The Fuck You Are shows you how to do just that.

Dr. Brett Jones is one of the wisest healers, facilitators and guides I've ever met. His potent combination of narrative, poetry, philosophy and wit will give you the insight you need to become the healer, guide and master of your own life.

Brett has the unique ability to connect the infinite to the everyday—and in doing so, show us how we can learn to connect to the unlimited resources inside of ourselves.

It is time for the new generation of creators, innovators and doers to emerge and step into power. Let this book spark the wisdom inside.

Daniel DiPiazza
Venice, CA
March 2019

DEDICATION

This book is dedicated to;

The suffering, lost, and dis-connected. Allow this to connect you to your INHERENT POWER.

Those that choose LIFE, every day, regardless of their circumstances. Know that every day you wake up, you are one step closer to realizing your greatness.

All the people who have challenged me along the way. Every time I overcome your resistance, I become a better version of myself. Thank you.

All the people who have supported me. This journey has had many lows, and I wouldn't be here today if it wasn't for YOU.

Kairos Training Culture. I Am because WE are.

The Source Chiropractic. I am truly blessed to live my days surrounded by the essence of this TEAM and all of the beautiful practice members that are part of it.

The Unshakeables. Your willingness to lean into these trainings are WHY this book even exists.

Dr. Danielle Cornelius. Without your effort & support, this book would have never launched.

Dr. Marvin Talsky. Thank you for showing me what true mentorship is all about. Your spiritual insights have forever transformed my life.

Kate Jones. You are my infinite Source of Love. Thank you for allowing me to be me and loving me the way I am.

My children - Jaxon Atlas and Willow Moon. You are daddy's inspiration.

INTRODUCTION

In July of 2018, a coaching group called "The Unshakeables" was created to help people discover their inherent power and wisdom. Monday-Thursday, I would wake up at 5 a.m., perform a series of movement-breathwork-meditation, get in a space where I was in contact with Spirit, then deliver a channeled message of awakening and transformation. These messages were recorded raw and unfiltered, transcribed by Dr. Danielle Cornelius, and now curated for YOU - to *Know Who the Fuck You Are.*

Each "Day" is one of the captured channeled messages. Several of the days have "Activations" which are designed to be read out loud like affirmations. You may build more understanding going through this book in sequence, and, please feel free to read it however the fuck you want.

We chose to SELF publish because we believe in the power of the collective and grassroot movements.

When you read something you love, please post to social media by tagging @drbrettjones with the hashtag #KnowWhoTheFuckYouAre

Your positive reviews and ratings will allow this book to defy the odds and experience EXPONENTIAL GROWTH & IMPACT.

All my Love & Blessings,

Dr. Brett

DAY 1: RESOURCES & RESOURCEFULNESS

"LACK" IS NEVER DUE TO RESOURCES. SCARCITY EXISTS ONLY IN A WORLD WITH LACK OF RESOURCEFULNESS.

When experiencing "lack" in life, many complain about their current state of resources. Whether they are not achieving what they want to achieve, or not feeling the emotions they want to feel, they blame it on the resources they "don't have." Most people are focused on what they "can't do." They don't have enough money for the seminar or class they wish to attend. They can't afford the life or object they desire. They don't have time. They don't have support. The list goes on and on, blah blah blah...

An estimated 815 million people are starving in the world today. Is it because we don't have enough food? Nope! Roughly one-third of the food supply gets lost or thrown away EVERY DAY. Only one-tenth of the world population is starving. We don't have a food resources problem, we have a food resourcefulness problem. I'm here to tell you, WHEREVER YOU BE, it is NOT due to your resources. Sure, resources will play a part in where you start, but your RESOURCEFULNESS determines where you are going. Greatness is awarded to those who are the most resourceful AND consistent in the pursuit of their dreams. Talent will only get you so far. And hard work always beats talent when talent doesn't work hard.

Resourcefulness is empowered by Universal connection and a deep understanding of needs. Say we don't have enough money, or we don't THINK we have enough money. That means you might not know enough people, or you may not currently possess the correct communication strategies to help inspire, motivate, and influence people. Money may not be currently in your posession, but the resourceful know how to get it.

Here is another essential thing to understand about resourcefulness. We live in a Universe that is continually expanding. We used to believe that what was set was set, and that's it. But due to the research of astrophysicists, we now understand that the world is continuously expanding. Not just our solar system, but the Universe as a whole. It is infinite upon infinite and ever-EXPANDING. If we have the mindset that the Universe is expanding, then the money supply is expanding, and the people we know are expanding, and the opportunities are expanding, the technology is expanding...

There are so many different strategies out there, you just have to GET RESOURCEFUL. So you want to go on a trip? I know people that have raised $3000, $4000, or $5000 by fundraising within a couple of weeks to do what they wanted to do. That money didn't have to come from them or their earning potential. It came from their influence and connection with other people.

Connection to people is very very important. It is through those connections that we will be able to become more abundant—and not just from a financial perspective but also spiritually. Some of the most spiritually profound experiences I've had have come from being in a group setting with other people with minds that are wanting to expand, journey and awaken.

So know this right here and now. No matter where you are at, it is not due to your lack of resources, it is due to your lack of resourcefulness. It is time to take ownership of where you are at right now and say:

I have not been resourceful enough. I have not connected with myself to the depths that I need to connect with myself. I am not connected with others in the way I need to be connected to others. I have been beating myself up. I have been believing thoughts that are no longer relevant and disempowering. Right here and right now I change that! Right here and right now I step into empowering beliefs and I step into my full power and wisdom! I express with all that I am and I stop. making. excuses. I am resourceful.

ΔΔΔ

ACTIVATION

Use the power of emotion and feeling in activations. I am using "activations" instead of affirmations right now deliberately. Affirmations are beautiful. They affirm life in the I Am. They are a great way to start overcoming disempowering beliefs. If you are having negative thoughts, you can affirm the opposite of those thoughts. If I am feeling weak at the moment, I can say to myself "I am not weak, I am strong!"

Getting into the feeling state is critical. Ultimately, it is EMOTION that is the multiplier, the exponential factor, and the quantum accelerator in manifestation. It is the FEELING state that is the attractor. We are not attracting the things that we want to receive in this life, we are attracting how we are going to feel when we start to reach new levels of success and new levels of understanding of our power. Go after the feeling! The beautiful thing about feeling is that your mind doesn't know the difference between feeling with your imagination, and feeling a feeling only as a result of an actual physical manifestation. THIS IS HUGE. Many believe they have to wait to feel a certain way (joyful, successful, powerful, etc.) only once they have had a certain experience in the physical realm. This is bullshit! The power of our mind and imagination allows us to feel what we want to feel in the here and now. And the more we FEEL, the more we are attracting what we want to experience in association with that feeling. IT IS POSSIBLE to live continuously in beautiful states and empowering emotions that attract the life of our grandest vision and most magnificent dreams.

As we commit ourselves to a purposeFULL life of powerful attraction, we will develop strategies, routines, and rituals to get ourselves into powerful manifesting states—and also be strongly supported so we don't burn out. However, I don't think we burn out from work, I believe we burn out from the resistance that is associated with not being in alignment with our purpose.

When I say "I Am" in the activations, I speak for the ALL, for "I Am" another name for God. In Exodus 3:14, Moses asks God what should he tell the Israelites if they ask for their name, in which God replied, "Ehyeh Asher Ehyeh." Meaning "I Am that I Am." No matter where you come from, you can start to realize the bigness of the great I Am. That which exists within me, also lives within you, for we are all interconnected with Divine Intelligence.

As we come into deeper alignment with ourselves, we realize that speaking in the "I Am" and being "SELFish" is actually serving the whole. So as I talk in the "I Am" during these activations, know that I am not speaking for myself, I am speaking for all of us. I encourage you to do the same.

In this moment
I am fully present and fully connected to
the depths of my being
To the depths of my Soul
I am getting in more alignment than I was yesterday
For my Soul's purpose
To utilize my talents, my skills, and my op-
portunities in the now
Meaning I don't have to be committed to the
things that I was even good at yesterday
As things open up and as new skills arrive
I put them into play
For I am here to contribute to a better version of
myself and a better version of this world
So I am constantly leveraging
My skills and my talents
To afford me the best life possible
I feel excited
Excited for this day
Knowing that here is another opportun-
ity to get just a little bit better

To live more in beautiful states of being em-
powered, of feeling fulfilled now
Not for something in the future but right here, right now
I am
I feel grateful
For all the things in my life that allow me to ex-
perience more love and more of who I am
The things that brighten my eyes
The things that warm my heart
The things that awaken my Soul
That right here and right now I can go through
at least three powerful images
That help me feel grateful
And as I feel grateful I am connected to now
And I know that gratitude is one of the best
spiritual practices there is
Right here and right now I visualize
The top thing that I want to accomplish
in my life happening
Not just see them happening but how I am
going to FEEL when it happens
Who will be around me?
How will I be celebrated?
What is the look on my face?

What is the change in my physiology?
And I allow myself to experience it NOW
As I experience it more and more and more
I am bringing it even closer to this physical dimension
It already exists in the spiritual dimension
It is already there
It is already organizing for me
I just feel it, and I feel it, and I feel it
And it feels good
It feels free
I am ready to experience it
And I am experiencing it now

DAY 2: PRIDE

PRIDE IS NOT EVIL. IT IS NECESSARY ON THE PATH OF BECOMING UNSHAKEABLE.

Someone sent me a message yesterday with a very religious tone. They told me how they believe I have a lot of power and that they love what I have done for their life. Then, they said they are sensing that I am not giving the glory to God and that there are "roots of pride starting to emerge."

I found that very interesting for multiple reasons, but I am going to get mainly into one: the negative neuro-association that most people have with pride. Think about this. When we celebrate pride in groups—gay pride, American pride, brown pride—typically there are not as many negative associations with that form of pride. But all of a sudden, when it is personal pride, people start to have issues.

The definition of pride is "a feeling of pleasure, excitement, or joy based on one's own achievements." Yet most people have a negative association with pride. But PRIDE IS NECESSARY. Why? Because our nerve system learns and responds based on the mental and emotional associations that we wire with it.

The depth and intensity of the emotions we experience will create the depth and intensity of our stored potential with memories. Memories root deeply into our system and produce energetic circuits and cycles that run "background" tasks, or programming, in our subconscious mind. These programs are continuously creating, attracting, and manifesting what we get to experience in this third dimension. If we experience success and achievement and do not give it any emotional tone of pleasure, then we have no positive associations to keep producing that success!

The human being is constantly doing one of two things: it is either going to take action that moves toward pleasure or away from pain.

If we are achieving things in our life in alignment with our purpose, WE SHOULD BE PRIDEFUL! And when I say prideful look at the definition. We should be celebrating with joy, excitement, and feel a sense of pleasure for our achievements. It is not wrong to have pride. If anybody ever told you it's wrong, they are attempting to squash your greatness.

A big reason that people don't fully step into their beingness, or become Unshakeable, or claim their greatness, is because they think that if they play full out, the world won't like them. See, while some people are dominated by thoughts of "I'm not enough," others believe "I'm too much." "I'm too much when I'm the real me." But guess what, nobody benefits when you play small.

I've had many people tell me I'm too intense. And, yes, there are times in my life when I can be really fucking intense, and, that is my AUTHENTIC VIBRATION. It doesn't make it wrong. It doesn't make it right. It just is. Everyone has their own specific and unique vibration, and when played in its full integrity, it is the most beautiful thing you could ever be! You don't need to be anybody else but you.

If you don't take joy in your achievements, who else is supposed to? And why the fuck would you want to keep achieving things, and keep having success, if you don't even find pleasure in it? I suggest making positive neuro-associations with behaviors and habits that bring you into more fulfillment and success. If you do not enjoy success along the way, then why would you want to keep generating it? Having pride in your achievements is powerful. It is powerful to enjoy the journey while you are achieving things. If you don't take time to savor, appreciate, and find joy in the moments of crushing your goals, then there is no reason to keep smashing them. It is powerful to experience pride, you feel me?

Pride is just feelings of joy and excitement for your achievements, and that is exactly what is needed if you want to keep having them. Again, we are always moving towards pleasure or away from pain. That is how the human brain, the human mind, and the human being works. When you learn to link positive emotional states with the positive habits and actions you want to reinforce, you will evolve into astronomical levels of success.

ΔΔΔ

ACTIVATION

Emotions are incredible allies in manifestation and attraction. They are the energetic charge. Words are just words that have a low impact without emotional charge, or tone. Emotions are what gives them energy. Emotions are also what helps wire it into the subconscious mind, which is the background programming that is constantly running. It is said that by the time we are 35 years old, 95 percent of our life decisions, actions, and behaviors, are dictated by the subconscious mind.

We may feel like we have a fantastic ability to focus consciously—yet research shows that the majority of human beings can only hold their concentration for nine seconds. We can train this lack of focus through movement, breathwork, and meditation, but remember, the conscious mind is only running five percent of the show. So, how can you better leverage the power of the subconscious mind? Create positive neuro-associations empowered by positive emotional states.

I am all that I am
I don't have to hold back for anybody
I find the truth in my resonance
I find the truth in my field and I express of it fully
Continuously
Relentlessly
Because I know I was born for greatness
And I do myself and the world a disser-
vice by not being great
I take pride in my achievements
I take pride in all that I already am
Not all that I have to become
For what I am now is enough and I feel
it with all of my being
I am ready to contribute to myself and to con-
tribute to this world today
It is OK to be selfish because what evolves
is the perception of Self
I know SELF is All and if I don't love myself,
and if I don't help heal myself,
I can't do it for anybody else
And how is anybody else supposed to, if I am
a microcosm of the Universe?
So yeah I put SELF first today and all of what SELF means

And I am excited
I am excited for this day!

DAY 3: MOMENTUM

THE CRUCIAL FACTOR OF EXPONENTIAL GROWTH.

Momentum wields the power to create exponential growth in your life. You are an expression of what your standards are for yourself. Get in the habit of going ALL-IN. When you go ALL-IN, you can create momentum, and momentum is like an avalanche—a snowball that becomes a massive force of nature under the right circumstances.

Now, that is a cool visual and all, but the other thing I have learned about momentum is when you actually start hitting momentum, it scares the shit out of you. There is a tendency to do a few small things toward your growth, then when the Universe opens up and really starts to provide what you are attracting and taking action on, you can feel like, "whoa, hold on, slow this shit down Universe!"

You don't have to slow down. You don't have to be scared. What you need is to trust in yourself and to energize your environment and surroundings —which also means people—to be of the same energy.

It is common that the people closest to you will be NON-supportive of your momentum. Yeah, you heard that right. They would prefer you to stay the same, just like them. When you are not feeling supported, it is easy to start closing down your creative potential. However, you do not need to be a victim to the perception of a non-supportive environment. You have the power to alter the tone of your environment, shift intentions *for* your environment, and have the interactions that you want to have by expressing strong boundaries. **It is your boundaries and your standards that allow you to continue your momentum**. Excellence is less about what you do and more about what you allow.

This can be both an internal and an external thing. Ask yourself, "what am I allowing to emerge from myself? If I am getting the insights, and getting in the flow, how quick am I going to put a filter on it and stop it, or am I allowing it to go?" The other piece is, "What am I allowing from myself and/or the people around me?" A lot of times, we don't hold strong enough standards or boundaries for ourselves and the people around us.

That means that sometimes we need to check people, check ourselves, and check our environment for how we are choosing to interact with it. Because if we are on a path of monumental growth and momentum, then we need to make sure that our nourishment (physical, mental, emotional, spiritual) is supportive of our ideal standards of life expression.

Exponential growth is possible. A lot of people *think* they are spiritually connected, or that they have achieved a high level of "spirituality," but often when you look at their life, they are not creating or manifesting shit. **A great indicator of your level of spiritual connection is your speed and rate of idea implementation.** When you are genuinely connected to the bigness of who you are, you will be able to generate and create things in the physical dimension very quickly.

If you are not able to generate wealth, or attract the relationships you want to have, or cultivate the experiences you desire, then there is more work to be done. Usually what is needed is a greater state of allowing. It is a state of beingness. It is being truly connected to your purpose. Don't get me wrong, putting in work and "efforting" is also part of the process because it will help you build laser-like precision for attaining your goals. In the beginning, your focus can be more like an incandescent light bulb, spreading your energy in multiple directions because you may not yet fully know what your purpose is. So, commit yourself to do the work and allow the strain of your effort to refine your personal success and power. Remember, we miss 100 percent of the shots we never take. Be willing to experience momentary failure to allow for Spirit to emerge and provide the guidance necessary to evolve.

Allow the true SELF and expression to shine. Catch the momentum. Don't be afraid of the momentum when things start to open up. Have healthy boundaries and standards for yourself and the people around you, and you will continue to grow.

ΔΔΔ

ACTIVATION

Remember it is essential to get into the feeling state. You don't have to just listen to me perform these. You can do yours on your own. It is important to carry a vibration of whatever it is you are wanting to create, and speak these words into existence for yourself. Know when you are talking with the voice of certainty, with the voice of power, and with a voice that is connected to the wisdom within. Yes, be inspired by the words, AND put in the work and do it for yourself.

I don't reject fear, I notice fear

As I notice fear I remind myself of the power that I am

Of the truth that I am

Of the source that I am

That I have the power to reorganize the living Universe to be an asset to my life and to my health

The support that I need is coming in

The peer group that I need is coming in

The love that I need in my life is coming in
Not only just coming in, it is already here,
I feel it in the now
I own it with every cell of my being
It is resonating with this power, strength,
love, wisdom, and humility
I am a better version of myself today than I was yesterday
I will be even better tomorrow than I was today
I feel grateful for my growth opportunities
I am letting this momentum just build and build and build
I am not burning out because I am not hitting resistance
Because this is an internal thing expressing
I am allowing this greatness to emerge
I am peeling back the layers of everything that is not
And revealing all I am

DAY 4: HOLD THE STANDARD

WE RECEIVE IN THE VIBRATION THAT WE ARE. IF WE WANT TO RECEIVE MORE, WE NEED TO BE MORE. WE MUST HOLD A STANDARD GREATER THAN OUR CURRENT CIRCUMSTANCES.

They say in relationships, you don't attract what you want, you attract what you are. This same concept holds true in all aspects of our life. When I say "hold the standard" I am not just talking about your current standard. I'm talking about your potential.

One of the real-life examples I have for this is in relationship to lifting weights. If you approach a bar with 225 pounds loaded on it, and your dominant thoughts are, "225 pounds is heavy"... guess what?

225 pounds is fucking heavy! However, when you approach the bar at *whatever* weight is loaded on it, and you KNOW you have a potential for your body to lift something much heavier, even if you don't think you can right now, approach the bar visualizing and thinking "I know at some point with all the training and all the work I'm doing, this shit is going to feel light."

The original perception may have been 225 pounds is heavy, but if you know that with training you will eventually be capable of performing a 400 pound squat with ease, then hold the fucking standard of your potential! Visualize yourself being able to lift 400 pounds. Know your body is constantly reorganizing to the demands you are putting on it. Command yourself to be better, NOW. Then step your ass up to that bar, and guess what?! That shit feels light. Do the work, hold the standard, and enjoy the growth.

It is the same thing in life. When you start to carry a vibration and operate at a tone that is far greater than your current circumstances, eventually you begin to live that. A lot of people wait until their circumstances start to change to start experiencing the life they want to live. Fuck that. Live and express a potential that causes your life circumstances to change.

For instance, I am a chiropractor. If I want to see a certain number of people a day, I need to hold the space and the pace of that vibration. If I want to see 500 visits per week, I need to move, think, and express in the vibration of a 500 visits per week chiropractic practice. Whatever it is that we want, we must set a tone that is in the resonant frequency of who we must become to achieve what we want to attain. Don't just see things as they appear, hold the potential and standard for what could be!

A significant activity that helps us here is to visualize your successes happening and *how you will feel* by accomplishing those achievements. It is never about the things you will acquire. It's about how you will feel and who you BE in that acquisition. We have all had the experience of crushing some of our goals and not feeling that much different upon their completion. Why? It's not about the goal! **The reason you are setting goals is more about the person you are becoming along the way.** It's about the YOU on the other side of overcoming your challenges! Visualize that bad ass mother fucker, and make it so.

Remember, the human body doesn't know the difference between illusion (imagination) and reality. This means you don't have to wait for acquisition of material items to begin to experience how you would feel upon their physical manifestation and reception. You can feel how you want to feel NOW. In the world of Neuro-Linguistic Programming (NLP), we know that the state of our physiology has a heavy influence on the state of our nerve system. By altering our physiology and entering peak emotional states associated with how we want to feel upon receiving what we want out of life, we are literally priming our neurology for an abundance of success. Let's know our worth and hold the freaking standard.

Excellence is less about what you do and more about what you allow—and that is an allowing of yourself and others around you. If you've got a big mission, big dreams, and big goals, you have got to set a high tone and high standard and live that standard and sacrifice nothing else.

ΔΔΔ

ACTIVATION

I am so grateful for the opportunity to be alive today
I am grateful for the little things that a lot
of people take for granted
I am grateful for the ability to fill my lungs with air
I am grateful for an able body
I am grateful for a roof over my head
I am grateful for a bed to sleep in
I am grateful for clean drinking water
I am grateful for all my challenges
I know that if I am getting new challenges
I am experiencing growth
If I am getting the same challenges I am staying the same
Thank you for my diversity
Thank you for my dynamism
This life is so vivid and I am so grateful to be living it

For each challenge that comes my way I say thank you
Thank you for providing me with oppor-
tunities to get better
I am ready to step up to the challenge because
I feel the strength and the inner power and that
inner wisdom pouring through
I know it is not all on me
I am strongly supported
I am strongly supported by Source, first and foremost
I am strongly supported by my family, even
when I don't feel like it
I am strongly supported by my friends and my colleagues
Because I give, I love, and I serve out of
a sense of abundance
With no expectation of anything in return
When I am a person and being of service, I am served
So I also allow myself to receive
I allow myself to receive help
I allow myself to receive service
I allow myself to receive the gifts of this Universe
I am ready
I am ready to hold the standard

DAY 5: MEMENTO MORI

REMEMBER, YOU TOO SHALL DIE.

What will the record books say about you when you die? What will your family and friends share about you? Live a life worth remembering! **You will not be remembered for what you say or do, you will be remembered for how you make people feel.**

There is a concept called Memento Mori. It is a practice of reflecting on your death. Remember, you too shall die. I shall die. What will the record books say about you? I want you to *feel* that. What was that initial hit when you read that? What did you feel? Did you sense a little tension, anxiety, or worry? Or, did you sense certainty, power, and love? Did something bubble up from a state of sympathetic tone (stress)? Or did you feel relaxed? If you started to tense up and feel anxiety and worry, I would suggest that you are not living the way that you want to live or the way that you want to be remembered.

ΔΔΔ

ACTIVITY

Write it now:

What is the tone that you want to set with your life?
What is the way that you want to be remembered?
What is the way that you want to be shared?
Think about your family sitting around, coming together for holidays...
What is the story of YOU?
What are they sharing about you?
Will you be missed?
Think about this, it is important.
How is it that you would like to be remembered?
What qualities or attributes are people sharing about you after your death?
How does your legacy live on?
For the rest of the week, live your life like *that.*
How will you be remembered?
How will people tell your tale?

That will set the tone for the rest of your week.

ΔΔΔ

ACTIVATION

In this moment, I let go of anything that

tries to limit my greatness
When fear starts to settle in and tells me that
others may start to judge me
And others will start to ridicule me and tell me
I should tame down my power
And I should tame down my knowledge and wisdom
and I should tame down my expression...
I step **into it** *knowing that the world only truly bene-*
fits when I am authentic in my vibration.
And so every single day, in every way, I am
getting better and better
And I am getting better at knowing what is my
authentic vibration and I let it SING!
I let it vibrate until it vibrates my whole being!
It shakes me on the inside and that shake causes
action and that action is on purpose
I am in flow and have unsurmountable energy
I am ready to live my legacy
I am ready to live a life worth remembering
Today I go ALL-IN
For the rest of this week, I go ALL-IN
I am living a legacy
What I want in the record books is being expressed NOW

DAY 6: WALK WITH YOUR LEGEND

WE ARE THE ONES WE HAVE BEEN WAITING FOR.

The person who I needed when I was going through the toughest of my times, I am becoming. We can all be the person that we need. We can step into being our own inspiration in a lot of ways. By facilitating connection and love and healing for others we are at the same time doing it for ourselves.

We have already discussed the practice of visualizing your death and what will you be remembered for and what will the record books say about you. Today, I want you to think about your legend. Visualize that the legend of whoever you are is waking up right beside you. It is looking you right in the eye and saying "we got this." Live in harmony with your legend!

This morning I had to wake up at 2:30 a.m. to get to the San Francisco airport by 4 a.m. The whole time I am not thinking about the small me. I am waking up to my legend, and my legend is like, "*Brett Jones, let's go!!!*" I need you to start talking to yourself like that; like your legend is right beside you.

When you feel like you don't have personal or individual power, you've got *legendary* power. You've got a partnership with the best version of yourself. If you lean into the best version of yourself, you will feel like it is grabbing you by the hand. It is not pulling you along, because you are willing to do the work and walk right beside yourself.

DAY 7: THE UNIVERSE LOVES SPEED

THE UNIVERSE LOVES SPEED; FUCK YOUR IDEAS! RATE OF IMPLEMENTATION IS EVERYTHING.

Ideation is not creation. A lot of people get caught up in ideation. They focus all of their energy, intention, and awareness on how badass they think their *ideas* are. People will say things like, "I am feeling very creative right now" and I will ask, "OK, well what did you do?" and they will say "I'm feeling creative in this idea or thinking about doing this" and I will say "if you are thinking about it, you ain't creating shit, you are ideating".

The creating part requires expression. Creation has to make its way to the third dimension, physical reality. If you are ideating, you are still stuck in the ethereal, fourth dimension. Start to bring it in.

A lot of us get great ideas, but we are slow to implement them. When you are slow to implement, you think you have a fantastic idea, but you sit on it. Then, all of the sudden, you see someone else doing exactly what you thought you would do!

Here is the thing. When it drops into the field of intelligence, it drops in for everyone. Your rate of success will be based on your rate of implementation. If you are being delivered ideas that you believe are coming from Source, you MUST TAKE ACTION. For those of you who think you have great ideas, I say fuck your ideas! Put it into play!

People hold onto their precious ideas because they think "this is the one" and "it has to be perfect before I get started," and three years later, they haven't done anything. Here is the beautiful thing about Source, getting drop-ins, and being connected... if you implement quickly upon reception, you will continue to be delivered even BETTER ideas! **The goal is to stay in an infinite flow with Universe like a torus.** If you start to mentally strain that which is being delivered from Soul or Spirit, you are subconsciously communicating you do not trust the higher power. Without trust, there cannot be the clarity of the Intelligence wanting to LIVE THROUGH YOU. Don't clog up the flow with your educated constipated bullshit! Trust what is being delivered is for your highest good, within divine law, and divine love.

ΔΔΔ

ACTIVATION

It is good to do these on your own. The key is to get into a *feeling* state. It is not the words that you say, it is the *charge* behind the words that start to re-organize the living Universe to come into greater potential for our action and expression. Trust the process. Implementation takes bravery and vulnerability. They are one and the same.

This is a key point. Make sure that you are honoring the feminine and masculine in the process. When I say take action, you also need *sensual acuity*. You must become aware of your surroundings, so you do not get too rigid in implementation. Listen, and then implement. Eventually, you will learn how both listening and doing can co-exist in a sacred dance of adaptive and dynamic creation.

Today I feel an ultimate alignment with

what my Soul is calling for

And as it drops in its little messages and little reminders and insights

Not only do I listen and ponder and contemplate

but I activate and put it into action

That is how I build a strong relationship to this Soul

I listen AND I am willing to express it

If I don't express it, I am saying I am not taking your advice anymore

Even if that is subconsciously

So I listen and I MOVE
I activate and I stay soft enough in the process so that I can listen
And can continue listening, and listen for the adaptation and integration cues
I feel amazing in this process
A smile is on my face knowing that I have a best friend within
And this best friend is continuously communicating with me
I am building better and better trust, more and more respect coming from my expressions
The Universe loves speed, so, today, I move with the Universe

DAY 8: THE SOUND OF THE SOUL

KNOW THY SOUL! WHAT IS THE DIFFERENCE BETWEEN MESSAGES FROM YOUR SOUL & MESSAGES FROM THE EDUCATED MIND & EGO?

Being in alignment with your Soul is like the being in the Eastern Australian Current "EAC" in the movie *Finding Nemo* (the scene with the sea turtles riding the super speed ocean highway). When you get into that stream, it's just GO! You are going faster than you ever thought you could, and you are stronger than you ever thought possible. When you are connected to your Soul purpose, and in times of expansion, it can feel like being in a slingshot. You will know when you are in it because you will feel like there is momentum propelling you forward from behind.

There are indicators to help you know if you are getting messages from the Universal Field of Intelligence and/or your Soul/Innate Intelligence versus the educated mind. The field holds and suspends ALL Intelligence. The educated mind is the *limited mind* even though we typically like to give it a lot of credit because the ego wants to feel important and "smart." However, the educated mind only knows what it has seen, what it has read, and what it has recorded from past experiences of *this lifetime.*

Our Soul has existed since existence. Its Intelligence is far superior to the *limited mind.* Our body will come and go, but our Soul is infinite and timeless. It was here before we were born, and will be here far after we are gone. When we connect to SOULular Intelligence, we are gathering the wisdom of each life it has lived prior to our carnal manifestation.

How do you start to connect to something much greater than yourself and tap into the infinite? You have got to understand what the educated voice sounds like. We all have it! We all experience the "chatter." That incessant chatter is often called the "monkey mind," and it's incredible at distracting you from what matters most—THE CURRENT MOMENT.

A beautiful thing you can do to empower yourself is to give that chatter an actual voice. A lot of people don't go this far. They know they have a lot of voices in their head but they never actually re-verbalize it out loud.

When you hear the voices in your head coming from your educated mind, causing you to judge and make everything rational, that is the prefrontal cortex. That is what it does, judgment and reasoning. When you feel that, and you are hearing it, give it a tone. What tone is that voice in? Say it out loud! The crazy thing is, it usually does NOT sound like your real voice. So, when the educated mind is talking to you, what does it sound like?

Next, I want you to feel it kinesthetically. When you are thinking about trying to create something from the educated mind, there is usually a little bit of a strain on the forehead right above the eyebrows. It is a little bit of pressure that you can actually feel when you are aware of it. When an idea drops in from the educated mind, it is like curtains from a movie theater are pulling horizontally across your face. You are trying to generate a solution, and then all of a sudden there is a new stream of educated thought.

Our Soul speaks very differently and has its own specific vibration. Soul is an individual expression of Spirit (which also has its own tone). Spirit is representative of ALL (also called Universal Intelligence, God, the Field, Divine Matrix, Consciousness). Soul is a fragment, or fractal, of Spirit and is associated with ONE individual expression of life. The Soul has its own wisdom from its own experiences from the lifetimes it has lived before enveloping and surrounding your body. Yes, right now, your physical matter is WITHIN the Soul.

The Soul has a sound. This is your unique, authentic vibration—it is your essence. The vibration of the Soul sounds very different than the sound of your educated mind. When I hear the voice of my educated mind, I have observed that the pitch is often higher than my actual voice. When my Soul speaks, it has tones that are much lower with a grounding and earthy depth.

Ideas from the Soul also have a unique way that they appear into our conscious mind. BJ Palmer (the developer of Chiropractic) would call them "Thot Flashes"—and "flash" is an excellent word for it because IT IS JUST LIKE A FLASH. Instead of having an idea like a curtain being revealed and this slight strain on the forehead (educated thought), insights from the Soul and our Innate Intelligence feel as if they are revealed from the center of the brain and it is like a flash, a spark, an opening. Like the divine spark generated from the center of a medicine wheel. It is a flash of expansion followed by a flash of contraction that makes an imprint of insight and inspiration.

When you start to tune in to what Soul is asking of you, you are walking hand-in-hand with your Life Purpose. Your educated mind can never comprehend the grandness of who you are—AN INFINITE BEING! The more you lean into the connection with your Soul, the more will be revealed to you. You can and will begin to develop the psychic abilities, which we are all capable of—clairvoyance, clairaudience, clairsentience. You will be doing things you never thought possible. You will originate action with Unshakeable Power and confidence. You will accomplish what others said was impossible. Your responsibility? Lean into it!

Know that when you start to act as a partner with Soul, it will take you into spaces and places that are UNcomfortable. Soul will give you ideas that make you say, "How the fuck could I ever I do this? How the fuck can I accomplish this?" When the educated mind gives you ideas, it's usually shit you have already experienced success with, and it's comfortable. But growth happens outside the comfort zone. When the Soul speaks, it's calling for CREATION—to do shit you have never done before, and yes, it can be frightening. You are like, "wait, you want me to do what?!" Know that your Soul prioritizes whatever is for your highest good and generates only constructive forces for personal evolution.

Get to know your Soul's voice. Know how your Soul speaks. Know how the Soul delivers ideas and images. This is the thing about living Unshakable. **How does one become Unshakable? They live a life they know is more significant than their small, individual self.** You were born out of a need of the Universe. When connected, the Universe will start to direct and guide you in a way that you can benefit ALL.

DAY 9: NATURALLY ALTERED STATES

"SUPERNATURAL & SPIRITUAL EXPERIENCES EXIST ONLY IN ALTERED STATES OF CONSCIOUSNESS."

Supernatural and spiritual frequencies are always around us, we just do not regularly tune into them when addicted to the physical reality —experiencing life only through what we can touch, smell, taste, see, or hear. If you take a look around your space, wherever you are, this is your physical environment, and most are only experiencing it with the five senses just mentioned. According to the Egyptians, humans originally experienced the world with 360 senses.

Altered states of consciousness allow us to open our minds to other senses and possibilities. Recently, I watched *The Pyramid Code,* and it said something in a way that I had not listened to before. This is powerful. They said, "Supernatural or spiritual experiences only exist in altered states of consciousness." When having a spiritual experience, you are experiencing more of WHAT IS through a heightened level of conscious awareness. The doors of perception begin to open up, and new realities emerge.

Right now, **what you see around you is NOT the actual reality, it is a projection of a reality based on your brain's current perception and/or misperception.** You don't see things as they are, you see things as your brain perceives them. As you look around, your eyes take in information, relay that information to the brain, then the brain creates a projection of an image that you "see." Modern science will tell us only about 80 percent of that projected image is reality, the other 20 percent is being "filled-in" by our brain based on estimated guesses from past experiences. Even worse, if we have been through any form of traumatic stress, we are now living through filters of a misperception that distort actual reality even further. Everybody likes to think that what they see around them is the truth... it isn't. It's their perception of reality, and that reality can be altered.

One way you can begin to realize there is more outside this physical reality is by having spiritual and supernatural experiences. Having spiritual or supernatural experiences can be predictable and reliable with sacred and safe routes to altered states of consciousness. The number one way to do this? Breathwork. All Natural.

Sure, there are a lot of sacred plant medicines that can also take you there. Watch *Neurons of Nirvana* if you are interested in more about this and how these "hallucinogens' affect our serotonin levels and how we perceive the world. However, whether reaching altered states through breathwork or magic mushrooms, the principal is to break the addiction to the limited five-sense physical reality (ego death). I believe we ALL have psychic and "supernatural" abilities, yet the majority has yet to uncover them. ANYONE willing to do the work IS CAPABLE of experiencing more of SELF. The 360 senses that we had access to in the past, does not have to stay in the past!

Recently, I facilitated a healing session with a man who just lost his wife a month ago. When working with him, I put my hand on his heart space and felt a wrenching clockwise, down-deep compression in the middle of his chest, locking everything in. So I took my hand and used this clockwise motion to try to first of all, let him know that I noticed what was happening, and secondly, to attempt to provide some ease so we can get insight.

We are spiritual beings having a human experience and not the other way around. However, when we get locked into a hardened objective physical reality, it is hard to see ALL of who we are. In the quantum physics world, this lockdown into a hardened physical state is when energy is acting more like a particle, and less like a wave. In dynamic adaptability, we should be able to move and navigate through both wave and particle states of expression, but 99.99 percent of the world, or at least of America, is locked into the particle form. Why? Because of fear.

Back to the story. I have my hands on this man's heart space. He was lying face down, and I began unwinding. As I am unwinding, because I am being a clear vessel, I start to feel the depth of his loss, and it reminds me of when I lost my brother. So there I am, knowing that there is a profound loss and I am unwinding... and all of a sudden, messages start coming in.

This is where it gets interesting. We all have experienced, through shared stories of friends or ourselves, messages from lost loved ones. (My grandma visited me, etc.) The message being delivered for the man I was working with was that there was a need for movement to keep his healing process going. By locking it in, he was actually causing himself to NOT be able to feel his connection to his deceased wife. We do this with loss. We try to hold on deeply and tightly to those memories, and by doing so, we actually clog the universal circuit of continually being able to experience more memories and emotions connected with that person.

His Spirit was communicating to become a cycle, to move, to let it flow. That would actually bring in more insight, more love, and yes, sadness, but not lock it in. I communicated some things to him, adjusted him, and then he gets off the table and gives me a hug. Then, he's looking at me dumbfounded, and says, "How did you know? My wife came and visited me last night and said the exact same things you are saying to me now." I said, "If she can visit you, she can visit me."

We have more senses, especially from awakened consciousness, then really can be imagined by a brain and mind that hasn't experienced it. I am here to create an impression on you that creates a sense of urgency that you understand the bigness of taking action today.

The more you can naturally enter altered states of consciousness, the more you can rapidly develop in consciousness, become more aware of your senses, and be a more conscious human being that contributes to society. It's a big fucking deal. So how do you do that and how do you maintain it? Breathwork. Every day for the rest of your life. That's all I'm asking. It is worth it. The breathwork can vary, but you must do it every single day for the rest of your life. Deal motherfucker.

ΔΔΔ

ACTIVATION

I am grateful to be alive

I can feel that Spirit within me

Every morning I allow myself to get into a

state that is ready for the day

A state that is grounded, that is centered,

that has allowed itself

To enter altered states of consciousness
for spiritual development
For if I want to have spiritual or super-
natural experiences
I have to enter altered states of consciousness
I allow myself to push the limits and push the bound-
aries of physical limitations so I can explore
And in that exploration I gain insight
And by gaining insight
I can make adaptations and attunements to my
life and to better those around me
I am willing to commit to that every single day

DAY 10: IT IS NOT ALL ON YOU

WHEN IN ALIGNMENT, IT IS NEVER ALL ON "YOU."

When starting new projects and in the thick of it, it can begin to feel like it's all on you. I remember telling myself when I was going through a tough phase, "if it's going to be, it's up to me." That mantra can motivate people to step into action and trust self in the explorative process. However, it puts too much emphasis on the individual. I would suggest, if you are in right alignment, it is NEVER ALL ON YOU.

When you are feeling isolated in your action, you are getting stuck in your third chakra, also known as the solar plexus, which drives physical-plane expression through willpower. It is a very masculine energy and very popular in patriarchal societies that have linear processes of moving forward and "getting by just to get by." This way of BEing creates hyper-masculine expressions out of balance with their divine feminine. Activating the heart chakra and the three above it are the key to joining the almighty ALL consciousness. **To move from the third chakra to the fourth chakra (heart), one must surrender their ego and be willing to FEEL.** When WILLpower, transforms to willFEEL, expect to HEAL.

When learning to get in alignment with Soul and Spirit, you will discover your Soul has a unique vibration. We talked about this already from a sound perspective. Soul will also communicate with you through actual kinesthetic sensations. One sensation that you may be familiar with is the "gut feeling"—and I'm not here to say that your gut feeling is Soul—but ultimately there are going to be things that you experience in your body that have you lean towards making certain decisions. For example, say you are on a hike, and you come to fork in the trail, there is always an initial and natural "oh I should go this way" BEFORE your educated mind steps in to say "are you sure?"

That *second voice* (third if you include Spirit), is often the educated mind, the ego, that which creates the separate self and can make you feel alone in the hardened physical state. So, start to establish a relationship with your inner wisdom and Soul. Then you will find—and not necessarily in any order—the Spirit, the ALL.

When you get in true alignment and right relationship with Spirit and Soul, there is an incredible momentum around you that guides you through life. When you begin to feel this support, you realize it can never be all on you. Even when you think that your friends are not helping or your partner is not showing up for you, you will know you always have your connection to Spirit and Soul.

What an incredible feeling, to always feel in partnership. Even on your "own," there is still a collaboration happening between your educated mind, the Soul, and Spirit. There is a triune there. In that triune, there is incredible power. For those of you that might be feeling defeated at this moment or feeling extra anxiety due to lack of perception of support, stop thinking of yourself as a limited individual. Know you are the triune of LIFE manifest in physical form, a spiritual being, having a human experience. And in that trinity of expression, watch the fuck out because you have become Unshakeable!

ΔΔΔ

ACTIVATION

I am not alone

The resources, the opportunities, the strategies,

the love, the life that I need to live

Is being delivered in the now as I learn to get in

better alignment with the triune

I align my mind with my Soul and with Spirit
So that when I walk I walk arm and arm with
my brother and my sister
I feel that power and as I feel that unity and
as I feel that community
Even within myself
I am reaching out and I am reaching in and
finding new layers of self
To move forward and propel forward
And to feel led and feel guided and damn it
feels good to not be alone
If I thought that one of me was strong
If I thought two may be even better...
Look out for three!

DAY 11: EMPOWERING EMOTIONS

THE POWER OF EMOTIONS THAT EMPOWER US IN THE NOW: GRATITUDE - PEACE/PATIENCE - LOVE/PRESENCE.

Today is all about coming from a place of love and presence. I know many have been experiencing a lot of expansion lately, and personally, I just had a massive revelation on how our emotions impact our energy and creative potential. There are some empowering emotional states that pull us to evolve, some that push us to evolve, and some that have us appreciate exactly where we are. THIS IS BIG. If you can begin to understand these concepts, you are tapping into another power of the Universe.

We have already talked about how when we hold the standard of our potential, we can transform our mindset for improved levels of achievement. The example we used was lifting weights in the gym. If you are going to lift 200 pounds (or whatever weight), and you approach the bar thinking that is relatively heavy, then it is relatively heavy. There is something weird that happens with your mind when you know that someday, even if not today, but someday, you will be capable of lifting 400 pounds. You can say to yourself, "this frame, with the right work, is capable of lifting 400 pounds." Now when you approach the bar, 200 pounds seems light because it is only half of what you believe you are eventually capable of lifting.

"Holding the standard" is about becoming the vibration of whatever it is that you are wanting to attract. So, if you are trying to perform at a certain level, then you have to vibrate consciously and subconsciously at that frequency. This same concept applies to emotions. If there is a certain emotional state or feeling you want to experience, you can literally generate it for yourself by embodying and emulating all of the physiological characteristics associated with that emotion. You "hold the standard" of your most desired feelings and emotions. **Want to experience Joy? Act joyous.** So, what do joyful people do? What type of faces do they make? What's their posture like? How do they smile? What's the tone of their voice? Then, emulate all the physiological properties of joy. If you go ALL-IN, within a couple of minutes, you can actually change your hormonal profile to match your joyous state.

Emotion is energy in motion. If you want more

energy, you need to be willing to express more emotions! Joy and excitement are two empowering emotions that help *pull us forward* in evolution. Both are high vibratory positive emotions that radiate outward. Joy lives more in the NOW, excitement more in the future. Both can be used to amplify/charge our intentions with creative power. On the opposite spectrum of joy and excitement would be sadness and depression. If you are feeling non-expressive emotionally, being able to feel joy and excitement can bring the energy needed to break through patterns of dullness and mediocrity.

Certainty and power are two emotional states that create a massive strength that radiates from within and helps *push us forward* in evolution. To have certainty, you need to have clarity. To have clarity, you need to have a clear vision. You will know your vision is clear when it doesn't feel like you are having to continually ideate it. Instead, it is continually being revealed to you.

Next, I want to talk about are the empowering emotions of the triune. These really help you appreciate being in the NOW. There are three different levels of this. The first is gratitude. Gratitude tends to be sourced in the mental realm. In expressions of gratitude, we tend to think of what we are thankful for. By doing so, our conscious awareness comes back to our current state of what we appreciate.

Anytime you go into a state of gratitude, it connects you to the present moment. This can be a reflection of the big things in your life or the little things people take for granted. For those who think they have nothing to be grateful for: Did you have a bed to sleep in last night? Do you have clean drinking water? Do you have lungs that breathe? Do you have a heart that beats? Did you wake up this morning? There is always something to be grateful for, and the more you are grateful for what you have, the more you get to be grateful for.

Then you have patience and peace. I believe patience and peace are in the dimensions of our Soul. They have a calmer vibration that resonates deeply with our authentic subtle being. The opposite of patience and peace would be anger and rage.

Next, love and presence. Now, love is an expression of Universal Intelligence and that which is connected to Spirit. My mentor, Marvin Talsky DC says, "love is the cohesive nature of the Universe." I believe that's why people say, "if you love something, let it go." Love will always remain. You can strip a person of all their worldly possessions, their identity, and their ego, and there will still be love. To experience love is to experience the ultimate presence. Nothing else matters in the presence of love. It takes over. It connects you to ALL.

Gratitude, peace and patience, and love and presence are the three layers of emotions that help connect us to the NOW. The NOW is often neglected by people who are experiencing rapid expansion (stuck on the future) or contraction (stuck in the past). This imbalance creates a need for radical self-love and acceptance. The biggest lesson for today is to know where YOU are in the process. The better we learn to integrate past, present, and future, the more sustainable we are in the process of awakening. Remember, this is a momentum thing. The last thing we want to do is have big breakthroughs that are always followed by big breakdowns.

ΔΔΔ

ACTIVITY

Reflect on where you feel you are within these emotions and with future, past, and present. Ask yourself, "what is it I need now?" Take a few moments and go into those emotions that are most in alignment with what you need. Give yourself ten minutes, five minutes, three minutes, whatever you want. Ask yourself, what is it I need now and then allow yourself to *feel* that. That acknowledgment is going to be what you need to keep moving forward.

ΔΔΔ

ACTIVATION

Imagine you are getting the best hug you

have ever had in your life

That hug that just melts you

Just lean into it and just let yourself go

Visualize yourself receiving that right now
You have the strongest, loving support and
you feel it in your physiology
That feeling of just being held
Being supported
Know that your self-love is that support
Right now, I allow myself to feel deeply
loved and appreciated
For all that I am
I allow my vibration to slow into the now
which allows me to listen
It allows me to notice
As I give my system acknowledgment it is allowed to heal
I know that I deserve healing
I deserve love
It is ok to take these moments for now
There will be time to be excited
There will be time to be certain and powerful
But now I am in gratitude
Grateful for everything that I have
I am at peace
Knowing that everything I am doing, and everything
that I am, is creating exactly what I need
I am in love

I know that it is not all on me
I feel strongly supported by the triune, my
friends, my family, my community
Today I see the support
I see the love, I see the generosity
I am now

DAY 12: BE STILL

"BE STILL & KNOW THAT I AM GOD." THE SIGNIFICANCE OF STILLNESS.

For those that are feeling the busy mind and having a difficult time cutting out the chatter, imagine that your mind is a lake. When the mind is busy, it is like when boats are speeding on the water creating turbulent waves of distraction. But have you ever been on a lake at 5 a.m., before any other human activity has taken place? It's pristine and still.

When you first start trying to drop in—well, the first thing is to try not trying—imagine the chatter system in your mind as the busy lake. As you begin to quiet the storm of the waves, you will enter a dark space of silence.

The mind, when busy, is creating particles of light. Ultimately, light is what will lock you into one perspective. The objective reality that is all around us is dependent on light. When you remove the light, you remove the objectivity, and you enter darkness, which joins the infinite stream of consciousness. That is why I like visualizing blackness, darkness.

When the mind is busy, it is usually trying to bring me back to the ordinary physical cycle that I am used to, that which is comfortable. Even when it is not comfortable, it is more comfortable to have some level of predictability. We become addicted to our ordinary emotions, both good and bad. We become addicted to our ordinary conditions, both good and bad. We are addicted to the predictability of those situations, which are dependent upon light.

By stilling the lake, you are stealing the light. As we do this, we are allowing ourselves to enter the state of stillness. In the silence is where it becomes very apparent, what is the vibration of the Soul.

ΔΔΔ

ACTIVITY

Visualization

Close your eyes for a moment

Stack your ears over your shoulders, your shoulders over your hips, and just breathe

Usually, the conscious mind is projected forward because we live so much in the future

Because we live in patriarchal societies that
are obsessed with doing
But we are going to bring some dynamic
equilibrium to that
We are going to start to bring some balance to that
So let yourself lean back slightly
Allow that conscious thought to become
a singleness of thought
Focus on the skin of the forehead
Focus on just feeling the temperature in be-
tween your eyebrows.
Thousands upon thousands of skin recep-
tors that are sensitive
to your environment when you bring focus
How much can you feel right at the tip of the forehead?
Then, start to sink into the skin
Sink past the skin into the fatty tissue
Into the blood vessels and the corpuscles
deeper into the skull
Feel what changes when you hit the skull
Then, there is this little layer, this menin-
geal layer of dura inside the skull
What does that feel like?
How is it connected to the spinal cord that

wraps around the entire skull
And goes all the way down to your sacrum?
There is this pump and rhythm and flow—some
would say the kundalini rising, the shakti
This pulse is from the tip of your tailbone and
goes all the way to the top of the spine
And wraps the cranial system
That is one whole system of flow
Then go deeper, go into the brain tissue
As you do that, sometimes it is help-
ful to take a deep inhale
Imagine again this consciousness being pulled back
Then start to focus your intention behind your eyeballs
How can you withdraw your eyes back into
your head, back into the eye socket
And behind the eye socket, again into the
brain tissue, and just keep going
Imagine that lake becoming still, and that lake is the brain
Steal the light
Think about one silver thread that is at the center
of the brain, near the pineal gland
Think about this one single thread being con-
nected with the Universe
How do you have to slightly transform your sys-

tem to just feel that thread of connection
Now that thread is a guitar string
You don't have to pluck it, it is already vibrating
What does that feel like in your system?
What does that feel like in your chest cavity?
As you breathe deeper, let out a sigh
What you will find is that in those sighs
Especially as they become more authentic
Each and every one of us has an authentic sigh
That will connect with different parts of your system
Allow for the release and you can heal your sys-
tem from knowing more of who you are

"Be still and know that I Am God." What an amazing quote that is deepening in understanding here in this moment. For "I Am" is the name of God. Ehyeh Asher Ehyeh, "I am that I am." **Being still we discover the I Am within**. The I Am within is part of the intelligence that has lived through eons of time.

In patriarchal societies like in the US, and really the majority of the world, I can guarantee, there is not a lack of doing. If you are not hitting the achievements and success that you want in your life, it's rarely because you are not doing enough. It is because you are not in right alignment with what you are doing. Right alignment in the doing comes from understanding the vibration of your Soul, the vibration of Spirit, and allowing that to guide you. When that guides you, that is when you are working with a greater intelligence and greater wisdom than the educated mind.

The educated mind only knows what it knows in this lifetime. Do you want to trust one lifetime, or do you want to trust thousands of lifetimes? The creation of the cosmos is in our DNA. There is a wisdom that is within us and surrounds us. Are you allowing yourself to connect to it? "Be still and know that I Am God." You are God. We are God.

ΔΔΔ

ACTIVATION

Today I let myself connect authentic-
ally to ALL of who I am
By doing so I am joined by the creative
forces of the Universe
By doing so I become in right alignment
And in right alignment "the doing" is in flow
I allow myself to be in flow today
Work is fun when I am in the flow so I am
in the flow and work is fun

DAY 13: CLEANSE FOR SPIRIT TO MOVE

CLEAN YOUR SPACE FOR SPIRIT TO MOVE THROUGH—A LESSON FROM THE RASTAFARI.

Today's lesson is brought to you via a Rastafarian, and it is going to be adapted with current knowledge. I was on a service trip at the end of 2015 in Montego Bay, Jamaica. On location where we were adjusting, there was a Rastafarian that I got to chat with for about an hour, and what a blessing he was. This was the first time I got to hear some of the philosophy behind the Rastafarian movement. One of the most beautiful lessons he gave was how the Rastafari typically will make sure their house or their space is immaculate both early in the morning and late in the evening because that is when they say that Spirit moves through the building.

I hope I communicate the depths of this lesson. One, the external physical space that you tend to do your breathwork, meditation, centering, gratitude, whatever your daily practice is... it is imperative that it is held in reverence and it is a sacred space and that you routinely clean this space. In my space, I have is a large black gym floor, and I follow some standard martial arts rules. When you have a mat like that, you never let shoes touch it! Even when barefoot, you make sure to wipe your feet before you step on it. This last weekend there had been a few people at my house, so I woke up early this morning and cleaned my entire space to get everything pristine so that when I perform my movement and breathwork, there is nothing that is interfering with my connection to self, Self, and SELF.

The same thing can be said about your internal space. The same intention and attention you give to your physical spaces, need to be given to your internal spaces. What thoughts are you thinking? Are they powerful and positive? Or disempowering and negative? What types of foods are you nourishing yourself with? Are they creating clean energy, or indigestion and constipation? Are your movement routines creating freedom or dysfunction? How are you continually allowing *these spaces* to be cleansed, for Spirit to move through?

The importance of this lesson is BIG. There is a third piece to this. What about the stuff you need to do that you don't like doing? Yeah, that too. I tend to put off the corporate administrative things that aren't in my creative wheelhouse. But when those things pile up, they also become interferences to our Life expression.

Today is the day that you learn *The Magical Art of Tidying Up*, which is also a book written by Marie Kondo. Over the weekend, The Source Chiropractic was part of a street fair. In our backspace at The Source, we have an infrared sauna, and this ends up being the place where people put all their shit. It is that one back room or closet that everyone has, that doesn't have to be presented to everybody else, so it naturally becomes a disaster. Over time, this can become another source of interference.

What I am saying right now is there needs to be a priority of getting "clean" to the depths of you. It is your physical space—both the place of your obsession (where you spend most your time connecting to Spirit) and the place of your neglection (that one fucking closet you hate to deal with). It is also your internal space. What you will find is that as these spaces get clean, it is going to allow you to ascend more. **We can only fly as far as we are willing to root. Temples are not built on faulty foundations.**

ΔΔΔ

ACTIVITY

Do an investigation right now, mentally.

1. Check in on your internal space. How well fed or

well nourished is your system. Are you groggy? Are you inflamed? Are you stiff? Are you not digesting properly? If so, why?

2. Do a scan of your physical space, the spaces you most commonly use. How clean are those spaces?

3. I know you have one place where a lot of shit gets piled up, and I would like to suggest that you spend one hour today going ALL-In and cleaning it up. By doing so, you are clearing out the interferences so Spirit can move through. As Spirit moves through we are more in alignment and in tune with the triune and we take right action. **In the patriarchal societies we live in, there is not a lack of action, there is a lack of right action.**

ΔΔΔ

ACTIVATION

I am so grateful to be alive

Grateful to still be listening

Grateful to be exploring the depths of listening

I hear and I feel the needs and I fill them

I am in alignment with the depths of my beingness

I do the things that need to be done

Not just because they need to be done, but because I understand the depths of why

As I handle the things that I don't even
like to handle or delegate
It allows me more clarity and crystal clear vision
With that vision and clarity, I get certainty
And certainty is power
Not force, but power
So today I move from a greater state of power
Grounded in humility
Supported by love
I am now

DAY 14: THE MAGIC OF NOT FUCKING AROUND

OPERATE WITHIN THE VIBRATION YOU WOULD LIKE TO BECOME.

Very often, I hear people say all the things they would *like to* accomplish. Yet, they are still operating at the vibration of *what is* instead of *what they are trying to create or manifest.* Say we are wanting to create more abundance in a business. You are wanting to increase the number of clients on your schedule, and yet you are still operating as if you have space in your schedule. How many of us do this? Space opens up in the schedule, and there is a low down, and then you slow down! What are you communicating to the Universe here? "I'm tired, I need a break, I can't handle the volume, thank you for the slow down."

For example, it's 8:45 a.m., and you have some work that needs to be complete before your meeting at 9:30 a.m.. Then the phone rings, and the person you were supposed to have a meeting with cancels. Now, the urgency to complete that project by 9:30 a.m. is gone. Your next meeting is not until 11 a.m., so instead of the work taking 45 minutes to do, you leisurely get it done in two hours while intermittently scanning social media. Why? You lost the urgency and pressure REQUIRED to accelerate your efficiency and effectiveness.

I have a great personal lesson on this. My boy was a HORRIBLE SLEEPER. He would maybe sleep two hours in a row and was usually awake a minimum of three times per night until he was about eight months old. When he was born, I was in the start-up phase of launching two different businesses (The Source Chiropractic and Kairos Training Culture). While on my entrepreneur grind and massively sleep deprived, I remember thinking, "I wonder how much work I would get done if I didn't have a kid..." Sure, call me an asshole for thinking this, but you know damn well —all you parents out there—have had this same damn thought process. But here is the funny thing, when my boy was nine months old, he and my wife went on a vacation to her parent's house in Scottsdale, Arizona. I had the house ALL TO MYSELF. Do you know how much work I got done that week? None! I slept in, watched Netflix, took naps, and ordered food. What did I learn? Urgency is everything! We now have two kids.

The question you need to ask is this: **Who do you need to BE to bring forth what you desire?** If you can see the person you are trying to become in your mind's eye, with the attributes you want to have (which are your values), in what frequency do they operate? How do they move in this world? And YOU BE just that, regardless of the circumstances or the external environment around you. By operating at that vibration, you *become* that vibration, so you are *not fucking around.* There is magic in that statement.

When you are starting to feel worn down, there is magic to the not fucking around. There is magic in the empowerment of self. If you are genuinely connected to the bigness of the purpose of your vision, then you are *committed,* not interested. When you are committed you are willing to do what it takes. You are willing to be who you need to be.

So you can tell yourself, "It is Tuesday, it is six in the morning, and I ain't fucking around. Let's go. Let's get it! ... Now it is a little past lunch and, I feel a little tired, I've had a big lunch, and want to take an afternoon nap, but I'm still not fucking around ... I've got work to do and being to be." *We've got being to be.* We always say we've got something to do. But, really, we've got being to BE. Say it with me, "I ain't fucking around!"

ΔΔΔ

ACTIVATION

I am getting crystal clear on this vision

With clarity comes certainty
And certainty is a power
Not a power that I need to force
But a power that I allow
In that power, I can make bold statements
And those bold, catalyzing statements cause
a reorganization of self
And a reorganization of all
So that I can be who I am called to be
Where Spirit is constantly forming and re-
forming and organizing
I am a better version of myself today than I was yesterday
And that is the only person that I am competing with
And I am getting better and better and better
Because I am listening to the magic art
of not fucking around
I've got being to be
The world needs me
The best version of me
So I am going to bring it
And I am going to turn up

DAY 15: I AM ENOUGH

"I AM ENOUGH. EXACTLY THE WAY I AM."

You do not need to read another article. You do not need to take another course. You do not need to join another mastermind to become "enough." Right here, right now, the intelligence that creates and organizes the Universe lives in you! I have been doing some one-on-one coaching. It is fascinating to see the patterns that I believe we all live with. Many think they need to *do more* before they can finally accept the greatness that they are. We have a habit of forgetting about everything we have done along the way to get where we are today.

One of the sessions I had yesterday was with a new chiropractor who just graduated last year. He was having a hard time owning his value. Forgetting that he just spent four years in chiropractic school developing himself—and that program is fucking tough! Let's go deeper... I am not saying you are enough because of any level of education or really anything that you have done. **You are enough because of the Intelligence that lives within you.** We can learn to accept our "enoughness" by KNOWING WHO THE FUCK WE ARE. Some people will step into a knowingness from education, some through experience and others by an act of faith.

We only use five senses of an estimated 360. Think about that for a second. One of the most significant examples that I know of about somebody who fully understood that they were "enough," is a man by the name of Walter Russell. There is an incredible biography about him called *The Man Who Tapped Secrets Of The Universe*. This man was an artist, painter, sculptor, author, an architect, and was never formally trained in any of it! When asked how he was able to do this, he said it was from getting still and having conversations with the greater Intelligence. Talk about a person who was awake to the senses!

There are many documentaries about the mysteries of ancient Mayan or Egyptian civilizations. We still do not know how they did what they did. If you look at how the pyramids were built, we have a hard time duplicating that even with all of our modern technology—and they were built how many thousands of years ago? These beings were awakened to something greater to make the impossible, possible. One of the documentaries I recently watched showed temple stones that were etched in Mexico, and even with laser precision tools and the huge cranes we have today, we cannot duplicate what they created.

The reason I am talking about mysticism, or

whatever you want to call it, is because there is a power that resides within that when tapped into is far greater than anything we can consciously know or observe. This backs the statement that I am enough, exactly the way that I am. I don't need any outside-in stuff. That does not mean that I don't like learning new things or putting myself in environments with people that help me resonate at the frequency where I want to be. I am also a self-generator, meaning I am not reliant on the external. The external is a bonus. It is the cherry on top. I prioritize and rely upon that which comes from within. The drive inside, the connection to the Greater I Am. From that beingness, I will attract the people, situations, and opportunities that I need in my life. I will attract the environment that I need in my life.

When you do the work day in and day out, and you resonate at the frequency you want to be, you become a beacon and attractive force for that frequency. Everything that exists in your life is setting the tone for your interactions, opportunities, and your community. *I am enough, exactly the way that I am.* I am finding out that there is a lot more in there than I thought there was.

ΔΔΔ

ACTIVATION

No matter where I am I can be

Be all of me
I am grateful to be discovering new depths of me
I am discovering that I am the Universe
I am infinite
I am abundant
I am powerful
I contain multitudes
Excited for the opportunities that are appearing today
As I sink into my authentic vibration
As I connect to all of you
I know I harness the power of the Greater Intelligence
There is no greater power I know
So I am excited
I am ready
To carry the momentum
To hold space for more
Yet know at the same time, I am exactly
who I need to be today

DAY 16: MIND-BODY MASTERY

WHEN WE MASTER THE BODY-MIND, WE ARE WILLING TO GO THROUGH PAIN & USE A VISION OF BEING TO REACH NEW LEVELS OF OUTSTANDING SUCCESS IN OUR LIFE.

WHEN THE BODY-MIND MASTERS US, WE ENDURE GREAT SUFFERING UNTIL CHANGE IS A FORCED REACTION THAT LEADS TO A BREAKTHROUGH OR THE ULTIMATE BREAKDOWN...

If you really want to understand something, three things can help you learn better. One, you need to learn while in a peak state. Two, write it down with an actual pen and paper—there is something to the art of writing, not typing. When you actually write it down, you learn it better. Three, put it in your own language. You currently—based on your current level of consciousness, education, knowledge, and power—have a flow linguistically that makes sense to you, and that is in your wheelhouse. When you can take abstract concepts and apply them to your world through your perspective, you will learn them a lot better.

Understand that humans beings will typically move towards pleasure or away from pain. Also, know that the mind and the body are one and the same. If you master the body, you are usually having to master the mind, and if you master the mind, you are usually able to master the body. They go together like peanut butter and jelly.

One of the signs of mastery will include your ability to *enter* pain. A lot of people get this fucked up. I might even change what I said as far as human beings moving away from pain and towards pleasure because I have a different association with pain. Pain is different than suffering. What I have found in my life is that **pain is necessary for growth.** Because growth happens outside of your comfort zone. If you are experiencing new challenges and new problems in your life, that is a great thing! It is a sign that you are evolving. Often, it will feel uncomfortable or painful.

From a body perspective, I have noticed that if I want to get stronger, faster, or leaner, I typically need to undergo some pain. People often have a negative association around pain because we have been listening to what people tell us. What I have noticed is that there is a difference between pain and suffering. Pain is necessary, in fact, *mandatory* for the evolution and mastery of mind-body. Whereas suffering is optional. Suffering is the mental anguish that put on top of pain. For example, exercise. You could have two people that are going through the same workout, from the same level of fitness, and one is finding a way to enjoy the pain, and the other is bitching and complaining the whole time.

What are you affirming? Do you understand the depths of the *Why* of the pain? There is pain that will create evolution, and there is pain that will create a setback. One also needs to understand when pain is a proper warning that you are about to create damage or an injury that you have difficulty recovering from. We have a principle within Kairos Training Culture that you want to train 10 percent outside your comfort zone, on average. There are times when I train outside of that to 15, 20, 25 percent. When you keep it around 10 to 15 percent, you can properly recuperate from the trauma of the training.

This principle can apply to anything in your life. It does not have to be training while working out, it can be training in stressful situations, with communication, or anything in life you want to improve. Work 10 percent out of your comfort zone, without pushing too much farther past that, so you don't have to spend weeks in recovery. Say you enter a hostile situation and it was too much for you and you could not properly adapt. Now you are traumatized and damaged, and that can take years to heal.

Suffering is different from pain. Suffering is the mental anguish and our negative beliefs, associations, or disempowering emotions that we associate with pain. You can tell by the language people use if they are suffering or just being pained. Even this familiar phrase, "Hey I have to go to work." Or, "Hey I have to go to work out right now." If you are using that language, you are suffering. Instead, say "**I get to.**" "I get to go work out." "I get to go to work right now." *I get to!* I have the opportunity to! I have the opportunity to bust my ass right now! Not "I have to go sweat right now." You are suffering if you say, "I have to."

A sign of mastering the mind-body is when you are willing to go through pain and use a projected image of the being you are becoming to lead to your breakthrough. What I have noticed about breakthroughs or achieving higher levels of success, is often many will enter an altered state of consciousness. That altered state is the willingness and vulnerability to let go of where you currently are. What perspective have you locked into that needs a breakthrough to be the person that you need to be, to receive what you want to receive?

A sign that you are letting the mind-body *control you* is a thought process that believes you need to endure a lot of suffering and breakdown before you break through. Taken too far, the person becomes suicidal, and the ultimate breakdown is taking their own life. I believe that all of us know someone who suffered and suffered and suffered and unfortunately the suffering was never enough for them to change. Unfortunately, I believe the strategy of the majority is suffering from a breakdown in hopes of a breakthrough. They are willing to stay the same as long as necessary until they are forced to change. So they live a life suffering.

I'll tell you right now, If you are willing to do the work, and you choose to live *with* life instead of letting life happen to you, you need to be willing to go through pain. You need to be willing to vision something bigger than where you currently are. Something greater. A life where you are more fulfilled. A life where you will give more significant contributions. A life of continuous growth so that you do not have to be reactive because of suffering.

An example: Last night I'm at this event, and we did not finish until midnight, and I did not sleep well the night before. I still woke up at 4 a.m. and busted my ass in the gym, not because I had to, but because I had the opportunity to. There were two options in the morning, be willing to go through the pain of waking up to become a better version of me, or sleep in and continue to suffer in a sea of excuses and mediocrity. I picked the former. At 6 a.m., I also had the opportunity to give a presentation to a group of people, and it was the strongest I have ever been. It is not a mere fucking coincidence.

Why is that? Why is it that I find my breakthroughs and my ability to communicate not from the educated recorded brain-mind, but from the Divine Source of Intelligence? How can I speak from that Intelligence that has been here throughout eons of time to provide the wisdom, the words and the language that hits people exactly where it needs to hit them, to awaken their Soul so they can start to master their mind-body and live a life of purpose? It comes from willing to go through pain. That, and I hold a strong fucking vision for where we are going.

Whatever you are creating for yourself, be willing to pain for it today. Ten percent outside of where you currently are, so you have sustainable growth. You have an opportunity today. Will you take it? Will you hold the standard?

DAY 17: INSPIRED VS UNINSPIRED

GOOD & BAD ARE RELATIVE EDUCATED THINKING. RIGHT & WRONG ARE RELATIVE EDUCATED THINKING. IF YOU WANT TO MOVE WITH THE SPEED OF THE UNIVERSE, FEEL INSPIRED OR UNINSPIRED. THEN MAKE YOUR MOVE.

This lesson is massive because it is going to save you time and we all know that time is energy and one of our greatest resources. So many people get lost in contemplation of action trying to decide if it is right or wrong. Or judging others, believing they are right or wrong, or good or bad. When doing this, people get lost and miss out on the lesson.

Don't ever cut yourself off from learning just because someone says something that you don't agree with and then assume they are a horrible person. I will tell you right now, if you were only to take a snippet of something you did or said in your own life, acting out a behavior or saying something in the heat of the moment that you probably regret now ... you may hate *yourself* and never even listen to yourself again. I see this very consistently when people tend to put their mentors or people they look up to on a pedestal. When they see that person do or say something they do not agree with now all of a sudden they do not want to learn from that person anymore. They miss out.

Here is the truth. You could take any action in the world, and given the context, you might have a hard time drawing a definite line between "good" or "bad." For instance, most would say that violence is wrong. What if someone was going to harm your child? If violence was the only way to prevent trauma to your child, could you justify it? The lines can get blurry on right or wrong. Some would also say that threatening someone's life is wrong. There was a movie called *John Q* where the main character played a man whose son who was dying, and he had to hold the hospital staff hostage to save his son's life. That was the only way this kid was going to make it. Right or wrong, good or bad, it is all relative.

Relativity is based on the educated mind. We have experiences in our lives, and we get conditioned through our environment to believe certain things are either good or bad or right or wrong. A better way to think about this, everything is either an asset or a liability. My Sensei taught me this. I am going to take it a step further. Everything that happens in your life will either leave you inspired or uninspired. **When you think from the terms of inspired or uninspired, you are either "in Spirit" or disconnected from Spirit.** To inspire is to be *in Spirit.* When inspired, you are in flow, and operate at a greater state of efficiency through insight and intuition.

When you think in terms of strategy ("this is going to be good for my business or bad for my business"), or right or wrong or assets and liabilities, you come from educated thinking. Tony Robbins has a line, "when you are in your head you're dead." Trying to solve problems with an educated mind often leads to delay, hesitation, and generating things you have already done before. You want to move with your heart, your Soul, and your Spirit.

When you see or hear something, you are either inspired or uninspired. The beautiful thing about this is that it will also take away the potential negative charge that halts progress and evolution. For instance, somebody is charged about something negative Trump says. It doesn't matter what it is. Good or bad, right or wrong. People will say, "he's WRONG!" People love to go on and on about shit Trump says. But let me ask you this question, has anything changed in your life from bitching about it and thinking it is wrong? I'll wait...

Does anything change in my life from me complaining?

Does anything change in my life from me having an opinion and telling others about it?

Nothing fucking changes! But you are addicted to being right, you are addicted to your educated mind, and you are addicted to your EGO. But ego doesn't move the fucking needle. Take this scenario for a changeup. Trump is saying whatever he is saying and I am either inspired or uninspired. Now I fucking *move*. If I am inspired, I am more inspired to act from a place of intuition. If I am uninspired there is no charge there, it meant nothing to me, and I wasted zero time with it. ZERO.

That's it! How easy is this? It's a game changer. Inspired or uninspired. Not right or wrong, not good or bad, not even assets or liabilities. Inspired or uninspired and then take action. Imagine if you start to implement this in every aspect of your life. What changes? Your rate of implementation changes and the rate of implementation is everything. Let me give you a quote: "Success without fulfillment is the ultimate failure." That will hit many of you right in the heart because you are all about achievement but for all the wrong reasons. You are about achievement for the numbers, for the ego, and for what is right or wrong, assets or liabilities. When you lean into success for fulfillment and contribution, you live an inspired life, and *that* is the ultimate achievement.

DAY 18: BE THE IMAGE

I AM WHO I AM & WHO I AM BECOMING. WHO I AM BECOMING IS BASED ON THE CLARITY & STRENGTH OF THE IMAGE. WHEN I BE MY IMAGE, I AM WHO I AM BECOMING.

Just had the opportunity to attend Business Mastery with Tony Robbins, and Tony says you are in two businesses; the business that you are in, and the business that you are becoming. And they are equally important. That is just like the human being, isn't it? Every human being is who they are in this moment, and who they are becoming. Let's put that in the I Am: I Am who I Am, and I Am who I Am becoming. Who I am becoming is based on the strength and clarity of the image. Some would call this "vision," but I like "image" better because with an image you actually start to organize the seemingly abstract until a tangible mental picture.

Everyone has some idea of where they think they are going or who they think they are becoming. The more you start to crystallize the image and then take the essence of who that person is—all of their attributes, their behaviors, their habits, their patterns, their actions, their beingness, their personality, their identity, how they feel—you can then begin to live it. You can even name the image. Some like to give themselves an alter ego, an identity of the image.

Yesterday, I met a guy named Lewis Ford who also goes by the name The ANF Action Figure. You may have seen him on Instagram as @AllNatural_Fitness. He is the one who will be hanging from pull-up bars, and people will kick him in the abs, or he'll have a 225 pound bar on his back, and he'll be squatting, and in between squats people will punch him in the stomach. He does some athletic freak shit. He built his alter ego (ANF Action Figure) through a lot of pain. He went to prison when he was younger, and while there he was in solitary confinement for six months. When you are in solitary confinement, you are by yourself 23 hours per day. Imagine that—23 hours per day for six months. You don't see anybody. You don't leave the room. During that time something shifted in him. A lot of people lose their mind in this situation and enter a state of psychosis. It has also been said that a state of psychosis can be an altered state of consciousness where you tap into something different. Luckily for Lewis, he learned to channel that in a positive way. He realized that he had four years minimum there and had an opportunity to go ALL-IN. He chose to go ALL-IN on fitness.

While he was in solitary confinement he challenged himself to do 1000 push-ups in a row. And he did it! He did it and he passed out, entering a lucid state of awakening. From that moment on, after he did 1000 push-ups in a row in solitary confinement, he realized that **anything is fucking possible.** He did it through an image. The ANF Action Figure can take an "inhuman" amount of pain. And he is using that superpower to showcase to the world what we are all capable of. As a reminder, there is a difference between pain and suffering. When the ANF Action Figure is crushing workouts that would make most people cry, he has this odd grin on his face the whole time. He's not suffering. Suffering is the mental anguish that you put on top of the pain. As a lesson for all, whenever the image of the person you intend on becoming is significantly different than the person you currently are, pain will be mandatory in manifesting your ideal image. Pain is the indicator of growth! It is letting you know you are being challenged! And for every challenge you overcome, you are one step closer to who you are becoming.

When you wake up in the morning, I challenge you to wake up as the image. Because right now you may not like getting up at a certain time. You may feel tired. You may feel weak. You may not feel good enough. But I *guarantee* you that your image is fucking ready. **Every single day is an opportunity to close the gap between the person you are and the person you are becoming.** Channel your image and be that vibration in all of you—your habits, your routines, your patterns, your behaviors, your feeling states—all of it. If you need to name it, name it. But it does not matter what you call it, you will begin to know the vibration of that being. You wake up, you feel it, and you express it.

Within the last two months, something in my voice changed. There is a growl now. It is in me, and I feel it. It is the energy of my grandfather. During my last plant medicine journey, I experienced my grandfather dying and him wanting to give me his knowledge and wisdom, his bear medicine. There is something new the Universe is calling me for right now. I was talking with my wife last night, and she asked me, "What are you excited about? What is really waking you up this morning and pushing your drive throughout the day?" I shared with her that there is a new energy and the energy and intelligence that is expressing for me is different than what it has been in the past.

When I finished school and first entered private practice, I was channeling a lot of Dr. Sid Williams. He was all about being relentless and persevering. He called it "stick-to-it-iveness." That we needed "to keep on keeping on." That frequency was for the "Dr. Brett" that needed to get through the hard times. That was my channel of expression then. From there, I started to embrace this feminine, more spiritually connected listener. The Divine Feminine is powerful in a different way. Now, something new is coming. There is a charge to it. A charge of retribution. I know it is going to be fucking painful, but necessary. There is a charge of command, a charge of influence, and a charge of power for an awakening of consciousness. That is the new image, and it has a growl. And it is ready. I don't know what your image is, but it's time to close the fucking gap. BE who you are becoming.

ΔΔΔ

ACTIVATION

I am so grateful for all that I am and all
that I am becoming
I have equal recognition and respect and rev-
erence for both of these
I have respect for the image as much as I have
respect for who I am today
And I am closing the gap
I am so grateful to continue to listen
And to continue to be the depths of what Soul
and Spirit is providing for me
I stay connected to my heart space
I stay connected to my intuitive senses
I stay connected to the senses that are waking up
These senses provide direction and the image gets
stronger every single day that I lean into it

So I allow myself to let go of myself
If I want to be the person that I am designed to become
I need to let go of the person that I have been
Yes it is painful
And it is worth it
It is needed
And I am showing up
I am showing up

DAY 19: THE REAL ME IS EMERGING

WE ARE THE HERO WE HAVE BEEN WAITING FOR.

When you notice your bed feels good and warm, and you feel tired, and you do not want to get up just yet ... you are being a thermometer. The thermometer notices what it notices and reports back to you what it notices. The thermometer is necessary to help you know what the temperature currently is. We also have a mechanism called the thermostat, The thermostat sets the fucking temperature. Today, my alarm clock sounded, and I was feeling really comfortable in my bed, but the person I am becoming said, "Wake your ass up, and be somebody!" That is the thermostat mechanism in me that sets the temperature/tone for what is being called for me to step into. I set the temperature, I don't just notice the temperature and bitch about it.

We are the ones we have been waiting for. Sometimes we have to do some weird shit for the psyche. This mind likes to claim ownership. Ego loves to claim ownership. So sometimes you have to do some weird shit to take back what is rightfully yours. I want you to think about this right now. We all have that voice, some of us have many voices, or the same voice just talks a lot at the same time. I want you to notice, what is the dominant conversation? And who has taken control over you? Right now, you have to claim ownership. Sometimes you get stuck in past expressions, past traumas, and a previous identity. If you are stuck, your past has ownership. It is not what is real. It is not who you are becoming.

You can take ownership with some weird shit. I am going to challenge you to at least five minutes —and I used to do this for hours—but at least five minutes today I want you to speak one line over and again: ***"The REAL ME is emerging."*** Not my past, not the story, *the real me is emerging*. The real me is the hero. *The real me is emerging*. I am emerging. I am breaking through the darkness. The inner light is showing. The abundance is showing. And *the real me is emerging*. Pound your fist if you need. No more going back to the conversation that is not you. *The real me is emerging*. You are going to find new layers every time you say this.

I have heard stories about some of my greatest mentors and the shit they would do. And they are some of the most abundant people I have ever met in my life. One of my greatest mentors is Dr. Sid Williams. I did have a chance to meet him before he passed. There are stories about him. He built the largest chiropractic school in the world, had 17 chiropractic clinics, a publishing company, created some of the largest chiropractic seminars to date with over 3000 people attending in the 1970s. He was a powerful and abundant person. There are stories of him walking on the beach with people who were about to start a new school, and they would go into these chants with the same line for several hours while walking: "I am love, I am love, I am love." Going in, and going in deeper, finding new layers of what it means to be love.

It is a beautiful thing. I've done this. You lose yourself in the chant. This is part of transcendental meditation. You get a mantra, and you say it again and again and again. You discover new layers of it that help you transcend. For this exercise right now, it's straightforward. One line, for five minutes: "the real me is emerging." Lose and release the voice that no longer serves you... the voice of the past. The voice of judgment. We are stepping into taking control of this mind-body. Surrender everything that is not. Find the depths. Discover new depths. Every day is a unique opportunity to discover more of self. Being Unshakeable is about self-mastery. Once you realize the bigness of SELF, everything changes. The SELF is ALL.

ΔΔΔ

ACTIVATION

I am the one I have been waiting for
I am the hero in my life
The Universe is conspiring for me
Organizing for me to step into me to be
the hero in my own life
I feel a new strength emerging
I feel a new capacity
I am breaking through old boundaries
and yes, it is uncomfortable
I am breaking through past perceived limitations
and yes, it might be painful but I lean in
I lean into the hero emerging
It is here to save my life
It is here to save the life of my friends and family
There is nothing more beautiful than the authen-
ticity that is arising within me today
That is arising within me, right here and right now
All that I ever needed and all that I ever
am has been within me
When I get clear and have clarity it allows
me to be me authentically
I step into certainty and certainty is power
Within that power is identity and iden-

tity of the greatest SELF

Of the Great I Am

I Am

I am emerging today

DAY 20: CLARITY + CERTAINTY

CLARITY IS KNOWING WHO THE FUCK YOU ARE. CERTAINTY IS TRUSTING THAT YOU KNOW WHO THE FUCK YOU ARE.

Clarity will become deeper and clearer as you lean into the depth of the insight that you will receive from your Soul, trust what we call "drop-ins," and when you take the time to connect in sacred ways. Earlier this week I shot a video with Lewis Ford, aka The ANF Action Figure. Talk about someone who has received a MASSIVE drop-in about what is possible. He got his certainty in trusting the vision. The clarity provided a depth of knowing who he could become, and who he is. Certainty allowed him to trust that what was being delivered was on the money.

The one with the most certainty wins. If two

people enter a conversation, the most certain one wins. Two people enter a fight, and often the most certain one wins. Certainty is power. Certainty is what creates the world as we know it and the Universe to organize in our favor.

Earlier this week, someone asked me, “what is your faith in if you are not religious?” My faith is in knowing that my thoughts, focus, and energy are what create the world around me. Whether you like it or not, everything that you are experiencing is what you have attracted and created. If you do not like the world you live in, you might want to check your internal dialogue because the internal dialogue and how it is expressed in this physical dimension will continue to attract everything that is in your life. If you are experiencing a lot of the same challenges, you are staying the same. If you are experiencing a life that you don’t want to live, ask yourself, “why do you keep creating it?”

We have to reprogram this manifesting being continuously. Drop-in to get the clarity and connect to the Soul. Then trust that you know what you know, and that will provide insurmountable certainty. With that certainty, comes power, and you will start to create the world that you want to live in.

DAY 21: PEOPLE WILL GATHER TO WATCH YOU BURN

"WHEN YOU'RE ON FIRE, THE WORLD WILL GATHER TO WATCH YOU BURN."

Last week on Friday, I spoke at a chiropractic conference. Each speaker got 20 minutes. On Saturday, we had one-hour workshops, and there were breakout groups that attendees were supposed to cycle through the different available room options. I had two slots that were back-to-back with a 30-minute break in between. My room was pretty packed already for the first session. When I started, the room was already about 75-80 percent full. I probably had about 50 percent of the total attendees of the event in my workshop already.

Right from the beginning, I hit this incredible

flow. I was teaching philosophy, artistry, and applied quantum physics. Spirit was moving through me, and I was tapped in. It got to the point where I was about to go five minutes over my original scheduled time, and I was supposed to give people a 30-minute break. People were really in the flow with me, so I asked them if they wanted me to continue or if they needed a break. They wanted me to keep going, so I talked through my break. Now we are supposed to be done, and the next group starts filtering in and nobody left from my original group. We ended up with standing room only, 30-40 people were standing in the back. There was definitely a vortex of energy created in that room.

When I spoke on Friday the energy in the room was more relaxed than I am used to, especially coming off of attending a few Tony Robbins events. On Saturday, something shifted. It was another confirmation and affirmation for me that we will get out of life what we put into it. Because I brought the energy that I did—the passion, the purpose, the intensity—people were starting to respond to that and it happened a lot quicker than I thought

There is a quote I heard once, "When you are on fire, people will gather to watch you burn." That was the case. People just kept flooding in, and you could see their eyes were bright in excitement. They were being blown away watching what was going down. I bring this up, one, to share my gratitude about what this experience was because this is a message that I have been crafting and cultivating for a long time.

The other piece is that I believe WE ARE ALL CAPABLE OF THIS.

Ultimately, even if people disagree with your content, when you commit yourself to an endless pursuit of awakening, awareness, and increased perception by continually overcoming challenges and pain, your energy will draw a lot of attention with incredible attractive power. This power will at least help open minds, which is a Spiritual duty.

I have come to realize that I am never satisfied. The reason I am never satisfied is that I know that there is always more. I believe a lot of us feel that way. We know there is more. There is more room for growth. There is more room for expansion. There is more room for understanding. There is more room for evolution. Because of that, I continue to question myself and those around me seeking refinement and revelations.

Another thing I have realized is that constant evolution will be a result of your ability to be wrong. One of my favorite quotes is from Walt Whitman, "Do I contradict myself? Absolutely, I am large, and I contain multitudes." Most people are not willing to be wrong, especially when they put themselves in top-down leadership positions. You see a lot of that in chiropractic with practice management groups with one, maybe two leaders and they are always the ones that are expected to have all the answers and are never questioned are allowed to be wrong.

I find it necessary to put myself in environments where I am continuously challenged, pressured, and where I can be wrong. If I am never wrong, I am only associating with people who think like me and want me (consciously or subconsciously) to stay the same. In your own environment, if you are the top-level expert, I imagine you need a new crew or a new environment. Yes, it is an achievement of sorts to be at the top, but from there, you must find room for further growth! If you are too satisfied, you have given up on your potential.

It is critical to put yourself amongst different industries, with outside voices, for continual innovation. This will allow you the opportunity to increase your level of consciousness, awareness, and understanding, and ultimately, increase your energetic capacity. The thing you need to understand is that as your consciousness evolves, your adaptability increases. Your ability to adapt is in direct relationship to the amount of energy you are capable of distributing and being.

While delivering that workshop where people were flooding in, one of the most common things I heard in response was "you have such great energy"—what does that mean? We hear it all the time. What does it mean? What is that? If you start to understand and question it, then you will get more insight into what that is, and then you can discover ways to change your energy if you want.

You must figure out how to create more powerful energy; an energy that when others are around you, they just feel it and you don't have to say shit. Then when you do communicate, and you are coming from a place of certainty, intensity, love, vulnerability, and authenticity, it is deeply experienced to the point that it not only changes the people in your vicinity, it changes the people around them and their community. It spreads like a fucking wildfire.

ΔΔΔ

ACTIVITY

1. Ask yourself this question: "*What is good energy?*"

2. What does it mean when someone says you have "good energy"?

3. Define this for yourself. What do you believe your energy is now? If it is not where you want it to be, how do you start to improve it?

In the process of becoming Unshakeable, we are also going to become highly influential and inspirational. That is why we always reaffirm love, kindness, humility. The other side has strategies for manipulation. We have strategies of connection.

ΔΔΔ

ACTIVATION

I take time to acknowledge the depths of Self

Connect to where I am here and now

Allow myself to be activated to a new potential
A new potential of expression
Of life, of light, and of energy
I am more adaptable today than I was yesterday
I am reaching new levels of awareness
I remember to take care of myself along the way
I can always fill myself with gratitude, patience,
and peace and loving presence
So I am grateful, right here and right now for all that I am

DAY 22: PERCEPTION > SENSES

PERCEPTION IS NOT LIMITED TO THE PHYSICAL BEING.

Yesterday, I was talking with one of my mentors, Dr. Marvin Talsky. It has been a while since we have spoken sincerely about spirituality. It was very nice to engage with him again in high consciousness conversation. One of the things we got into was my current concept regarding elevated levels of consciousness being related to elevated levels of awareness, and these elevated levels of awareness allowing for more adaptability and greater energetic capacity.

In that conversation, we started talking about a few different things. One of them led to why perception ultimately takes priority over the senses of the nerve system. This is interesting because we perceive our world through the nerve system, and yet perception somehow has a superiority over the nerve system. Remember, we do not see the world as it is, we see the world as we project it to be.

We project the world around us based on how our brain analyzes incoming information in correlation with information that has been received from the past. Our past experiences shape how we currently perceive the world because our past experiences create a "reference map" of content that helps us more efficiently navigate the world. Unfortunately, this reference map can create gaps in what is *actual reality* and what it is we are experiencing as reality. It is like viewing life through a distorted filter that becomes more and more disconnected as nerves become more and more myelinated in their distorted pathways.

If we rely only on the senses of the nerve system, not only can we be living through a distorted filter, we are also just experiencing life as the limited physical self, and we are much more than that. This is where it expands. So how is it that perception has superiority over our physical sense organs? Because perception is not limited to the physical being.

When tuning into the triune of mind/Soul/Spirit, there is an ability to perceive *more than* what we sense in our physical reality, and that comes from higher levels of awakening and higher levels of consciousness. That is how perception can be superior or have priority over our physical sense organs. As we awaken, we will develop more sensual acuity and awareness.

Perception above and beyond the normal physical senses can be linked to imagination. Imagination from a human perspective (or physical perspective) gets thought of as "make-believe." It's not. It is revealing what is above and beyond the physical senses.

As one is in the process of awakening and developing more perceptive awareness outside of the basic five senses, they will actually start to *see through matter*. It is not that they are make-believing, it is that they are seeing what actually is. This can expand into your vision and image. The greater your image, or the greater your vision, the greater your reality. There will be a point in connection to Spirit that you no longer operate with a typical thought-process; instead, your vision is revealed to you. When it is being revealed to you, it is as real as anything you would see with your physical senses. It is not make-believe, you are just seeing what others do not.

Same with imagination. You will find that with a grand imagination, you are viewing things in another reality before they manifest in this physical reality. The more that you are connected to Soul and know Soul's voice, and know Spirit's voice, the more you will see that when an image is revealed to you, it is just as real as physical reality. Remember, as you start to attract in a powerful way, the tendency is to close down because it gets uncomfortable. I encourage you to stay open, to lean in, to turn the crank, and testify.

DAY 23: SUFFERING IS MISPERCEPTION

ALL SUFFERING IS DUE TO MISPERCEPTION.

Yesterday, I traveled for 24 hours. I was on a taxi to the bus station in Bratislava, then a bus to Vienna, then a flight to Amsterdam, then a flight to Iceland, then a flight home to the Bay Area. It was long, but I made it! In all that travel, I received some messages online, one of those messages being from someone who is currently experiencing night terrors. In response, I was able to ask her some questions that I believe allowed her to open up for new insight and a new perspective on it.

What I have started to discover through my own journey and the insights of others, is that all suffering is due to a misperception. I could see just in the tone of the message that she was feeling not only pain from her experience, but suffering from mental anguish to the point that she began to fear the dark. She was creating additional negative associations for why she was even having night terrors. So, I asked her, "What would it look like if your belief surrounding this experience was more empowering?"

This led us to a shift in perspective. She replied, "Now that I think about it, this is the closest to God I have ever been because I have been reading the bible before bed and I do think that there is a lesson here." She kept going through the process of discovering the lessons, and by the end of it, she no longer had the same relationship with what she had been experiencing.

I learned some of this from the book The Way Of Mastery. All events in our life are "neutral" until we decide that we feel negative or positive about them. That was hard for me to hear. I have definitely experienced things in my life where I did not feel neutrality. Losing my brother, my dad losing his job, my mom leaving ... all kinds of trauma. I have gone through some shit, and there have definitely been times in the past where I did not feel neutral.

In retrospect, however, everything that happens, as your awareness increases, only has the power that you give it. For instance, some people may experience something as simple as getting a flat tire, and that flat tire will ruin their whole day! And not just the entire day but sometimes their whole week, or the whole month! There are others who will experience the same situation and have no negative charge, they just handle it.

Yesterday, my flight out of Amsterdam to Iceland was delayed. I was originally supposed to have an hour and a half layover in Iceland, and typically they want you to board 40 minutes before departure. Because I was an hour delayed from Amsterdam, when I arrived in Iceland they were already boarding my flight. I still had to make my way through customs, and the line was hella long. There was a lady that was taking these passes that would allow you to fast track the line, I saw others from my flight in that line with these passes that I somehow did not receive. I tried to tell her that I was on the flight that was now boarding, but she wouldn't let me through without that pass. I knew that if I had to go through this customs line, I would very likely miss my flight, but I stayed cool. I thought, what is the worst thing that will happen? I am delayed, I have to stay a day in Iceland.

During this waiting game, there were definitely feelings of anger and frustration that were bubbling up, but for the most part, I stayed neutral! I knew I did not have any control over it, only the charge that I give it, and I had an opportunity here to perceive this as extremely frustrating, or I can just be part of the experience. Sure enough, once I got through the line, my flight departure time had passed, but the airline waited for the few of us that had got stuck. I made my flight, and everything was fine.

I am starting to notice that the exact thing you fear or worry about is what you create. I imagine the girl who has had her car window broken three times has a fear of getting her window broken again. I can almost guarantee you as long as she keeps that fear, she is going to start organizing coherent energetic particles for that experience. If I would have gone into fear and worry about missing my flight, what am I creating for myself? I am creating the experience of missing my flight.

That is not to say that challenges will never happen, they will. What I'm saying is, **perspective is everything**. It is a misperception that creates suffering. No matter the circumstance, you can always shift your perspective. Your ability to shift perspective is directly related to your level of awareness. One of the number one things we can do in life is to continue to find ways to increase our levels of awareness and discover more understanding for that which we do not understand.

For instance, when I was going through all the trauma in my late teens and 20s, the reason I was suffering so much was because of my lack of understanding. I had a lack of awareness of the bigness of what was going on. I was lost in the trees and could not see the forest. This happens to many of us. We get so put down by our current circumstances that we are unable to see the bigger picture. What we lack is perspective.

Think about it. Why do people, especially women, often want to talk to each other during hard times? They are looking for that shift in perspective. Why do we go to food or drugs? They change your chemistry for a change in perspective. There is a more sustainable way. It is making contact and connection to Spirit. Again and again and again.

If you are suffering right now, it is due to a misperception. In all of the struggle, there is always a lesson. So, how can you make small shifts in your perspective that allow you to see the challenge, to feel the pain, but not suffer?

DAY 24: 90/10 RULE

HEALTH IS 90% CONSISTENCY/HABIT & 10% VARIANCE/CHALLENGE.

Health is 90 percent about consistency (what you do out of habit) and 10 percent about variance and challenge. Most of us have heard of the 80/20 Principle in life where 20 percent of what you do gets you 80 percent of your results. This is used a lot in training, business, and other practices. I have found that health operates a bit outside of this principle.

For me, my level of health, vibrancy, and consciousness are mainly created by the things I do consistently—my habits. That is why it is good to be home. On my travels, it is a struggle to find consistency because I am moving around different places with various time zones. As much as possible, my food stayed similar-ish, but my morning routines were jacked, and a lot of things got turned upside down.

I believe we all need reminders and check-ins to stay on track to build life habits for health. When I was in chiropractic school, every quarter, I would write out an "Innateness Plan "for myself. The Innateness Plan was designed to create a framework that allowed me to dig into the four pillars of health: nourishment, movement, recuperation, and mindfulness. For nourishment, I would consider what I was currently eating, and decide on a specific diet I wanted to experiment with (Paleo, Keto, Vegan, etc.) to take my health to the next level.

From there, I would write out specific details about my plan. For example, when it comes to nourishment, what am I allowed to eat? What am I not allowed to eat? For how long would I be committing to that plan? Were there any days off that plan? What was the reward for finishing? What was the punishment if I didn't follow through? And the biggest question of all, why the fuck did it matter? Then, I would detail out the next pillar. With movement, I would ask myself, what was it I was wanting to accomplish with my body and fitness? Was I seeking power? Strength? Flexibility? How many days would I be training? And for how long? Again, the more detailed, the better. I structure it all out. For mindfulness, I considered what type of meditation and breathwork I wanted to explore. For how long? How many days a week? What days that week and at what times? What is the level of presence and focus I'm wanting to obtain?

Then, the next pillar, recreation and recuperation. This is the one that is usually lacking for the majority of us. There are two primary forms of recuperation/recreation, active and passive. Active forms include activities you are doing yourself (rolling, stretching, hiking, etc.) Passive forms include services you are receiving (chiropractic, cryo, infrared sauna, bodywork, acupuncture, etc.)

At this phase in my life, I am getting acupuncture every other week, craniosacral every other week, and chiropractic about once a week. I do movement/mobility/stretching every day, followed by breathwork and meditation in an infrared sauna. That is my current formula, but it always changes. It is essential to have these check-ins regularly to see how our habits are creating expressions of health and function, or sickness and dysfunction. **Whether you like it or not, I can guarantee you it's your habits that are creating your life expression.** So, what do you like and/or not like about your habits?

For some history, I finished my football career in 2008, and I was beaten up. My shoulders were so jacked that I could no longer do overhead presses without a considerable amount of pain. Even attempting to do pulls from overhead were uncomfortable for a long time. For years I avoided performing strength and power activities in fear of further damage and injury. This really fucked with my psyche because my entire life was built around strength and power for athletic performance. It was not until this year that I finally started programming more intense strength and power exercises back into my routine. That was a 10 year process recovering from the trauma of football to enter this phase where I am finally able to perform again. I listened to my body, many people do not.

Some people come into my office experiencing being victim or slaves to a former ideology of expression that is out of integrity with who they are now. For example, I take care of one lady who is experiencing a lot of pain and suffering due to her commitment to Crossfit. When I check her system and listen to her deeply, I notice her body is requesting movement that is more gentle and fluid. It's not that there's anything wrong with Crossfit, her body is just not asking for that right now. So, I tell her, "your system, is requesting more love, compassion, flexibility, and less of these bigger, faster, and heavier movements." And if she really listens in, she could acknowledge that for herself and avoid the suffering and agony of the conflicted ego.

So, how much are we willing to honor and nurture ourselves for where we are at now? I am not saying do not commit to something and challenge yourself, because again, 10 percent is the challenge. **Ninety percent of your health will come from your habits, 10 percent will come from the variance.** This is an applied theory based on what I am currently experiencing. I feel like 80/20 gives you too much wiggle room.

For a long time, I did the Innateness Plan every quarter, but after so many repetitions, I began to sense my needs without having to rely on going through the exercise itself. A lot more adaptation happens for me on the go now. However, if you are just getting started on this journey, I can't recommend it enough.

ΔΔΔ

ACTIVITY

1. Write down the four pillars of health: movement, nourishment, recuperation, mindFLOWness.

2. Take a look and grade yourself on how you feel you are doing in each of these four pillars. Look at where you are now, what you have been doing, what is working and what is not, and where would you like to see more improvement in each category.

3. Set a time limit, like three weeks or 21 days.

4. Based on where your at and potential voids you are noticing, create a three week plan for yourself for each pillar. Write down what you want to do for the next 21 days.

5. For each of these things also consider *why*. Example, when I have a better movement practice, and I am more agile and mobile, I can wrestle these damn kids! For me, that is important because I want to have energy that is sustainable and that helps me show up in business and with my family. How do I create

health and abundance so I can be those things? For yourself, look for a deep-rooted *Why* and write up a plan.

6. Then you are going to hold yourself accountable. Tell people you are doing this if it helps.

Look at your habits. Because 90 percent of your habits are creating your state of health. When it comes to the voids you notice, also focus on the beauty that you notice. We can let our deficiencies drag us down or inspire us because that is room for growth. I love seeking out and finding imperfections because I don't feel negative about them. I look at my flaws and say to myself, "Sweet. There is an area I can put some love into, and an area I'm going to improve."

ΔΔΔ

ACTIVATION

I Am deeply, deeply grateful to be alive today

Always learning

Learning more about myself

The "good" and the "bad"

Just noticing

Noticing any particular trends or cycles

And how they may or may not relate to universal cycles

Allowing myself to be a better listener today

And also willing to take action
I am of the vibration of that which I am becoming
The vision is getting clearer and clearer
I feel grateful for everything I have in my life now
That gratitude fills me up and fuels me up
I feel the peace and the surrender
I feel the love and the presence
The certainty and the power
Bringing me forward with a clear vision, being tapped-in and connected to Source
I am grateful to start my day this way
I will allow this feeling, expression, and experience to continue throughout my day
And extend to those that I have the opportunity to meet and greet and connect with
I am attracting the people and the opportunities that I need to become the best self possible

DAY 25: SOCIAL MEDIA IS BUSINESS

THE KEY TO BREAKING THROUGH THE PITFALLS OF SOCIAL MEDIA IS UNDERSTANDING IT IS BUSINESS. THE TWO KEYS TO BUSINESS: 1) DYNAMIC INNOVATION & 2) VALUE BASED MARKETING

I am going to be really honest, I have been struggling. Mainly with this whole social media thing. I have my moments where I am very anti. Because I notice what I notice when I am on social media. What I notice from some of the people and contributors on social media, is how easy it is to become enslaved to it. I think most people are aware of this, but I think a lot of people don't see the other aspects of it.

There are levels to this. For instance, a lot of these more prominent practice management groups within chiropractic, and within other various industries, will have online groups with weekly meetings, weekly lessons, follow-up lessons, Q&A's, breakout groups, one-on-ones, and other various online time commitments. Which means, of course, if you are playing the game, you end up on the phone or in front of your laptop all the damn time! I don't know about y'all, but the "laptop lifestyle" ain't the life I dream up for myself. I am in this to live! I am in this because I want to feel alive!

So how is it that one can provide enough value and insight for others while creating an equal amount of value and love for self? There has got to be another way besides hours upon hours interacting with a device. I have been trying to think my way through this, and that is where I went wrong. "If you are in your head, you're dead." I keep analyzing and trying to get creative with my educated mind, and we've already discussed the limitations of the educated mind. I was in the sauna today and told myself, "Dude! Do what you tell everyone else to do and breathe motherfucker!

So I go IN on the breathwork this morning. I was pushing my boundaries, getting the vibration going, and developing the "pineal shakes." Then a question popped into the field, I had to ask myself, "do I really want to do all of this?" I have my moments where I say "fuck it" and want to get off social media altogether. And I know I am not the only one that feels this way. It is a very interesting world we are living in right now. It is so easy to lose yourself in technology. **We must create healthy boundaries for how we show up and interact in the digital space.** As awakening human beings, we have a duty and obligation to leave this world better than we found it. In all ways, always.

So I am trying to work my way through this in the sauna today when I am breathing, and I realize, it's just business. People on social media are in business. The marketers, the advertisers, the content-creators, those launching content, those that are tracking their engagement and reach to increase viewership continually ... all of it is business.

If you are in this game, you are in business for yourself. Even if you do not think you have a business, you are building business potential. Why do people give a shit about how many likes and follows they receive? If it is not for current business, it is for the potential of future business. Those that are in the know, know that followers can turn into customers. It is a new form of digital currency. Now don't get me wrong, I am quite aware that many interact with social media purely for keeping in touch with family and friends. And, for those that are stepping into their power, know that this world needs leaders of positivity and transformation. Just by reading this book, you are that! If you have life lessons to share, you have value! And that value can be monetized, whenever you are ready.

Now that you may be realizing your business potential, what are the keys for a business to be healthy? Constant dynamic innovation and marketing. Today, social media is basically an opportunity for social marketing of who you are, who you be, and the services you provide. I do think it can be done principally and congruently with a lifestyle that honors the life that you want to live. A perspective shift that is helping me at this moment is to know that for every piece of content I create for social media, I am increasing my business potential and perceived value.

When people think "business," they think "money," and then often associate business as "evil" or "bad." Why? Because we are brainwashed with concepts of how influential business people often only think about themselves, and that is a disempowering misperception. There are people in this world that are creating businesses that give other people good jobs that help them provide for their families. There are businesses that offer services that honor and nurture the development and evolution of the world.

I have had many conversations in my social circles about the concept of money. A lot of people have a negative connotation with money because typically when they see money, and they see people that have power with money, they are used to seeing it used in sinister ways. But that is not the whole truth. Money is an energy that can be used; however you want to use it—for philanthropy, for movements, social justice, it can be used for anything.

If you want to be strong in business—and business is what you make it—you must constantly innovate for your customer. Let me say that again, you are innovating for your customer. To innovate for your customer, you need to know your customer. One of the ways to achieve that understanding is by knowing your social media engagement. What types of posts are people most interacting with? This will give you insight into what your audience wants. If you are unsure, you can always ask. “Hey Y'all, what was it you liked about this post or video? How could it be better to bring you even more value?”

The second key to success in business is marketing. Grant Cardone says, “obscurity is the single the biggest killer to a business or entrepreneur.” I agree, obscurity is one of the biggest reasons I see chiropractors fail in practice. **There are far too many phenomenal chiropractors that have an amazing service to offer humanity, but don't see anybody! The problem is not their product or service, the problem is obscurity.** Nobody knows who they are and how to find them. At this moment, one of the better ways to become more known is with proper use of social media.

I had to go “dark” today to learn this lesson. Entering an altered state of consciousness through breathwork allows one to escape the cyclic pattern of the educated mind addicted to the light objective reality. See, all creation is birthed from a dark space. The Universe was birthed out of a black hole, and humanity is birthed out of the womb ... another black hole. Sometimes it is necessary to travel to these dark spaces and places to grab the insight we need for empowering perspective shifts in our life. I am at better terms now with social media because I realize it is part of being in business. Being willing to venture to these spaces may help you understand why social media is here for you. Just do not get lost in it. *Remember who the fuck you are.*

ΔΔΔ

ACTIVATION

I am who I am
I stand strong in who I am and who I be
I listen to my internal and external environment
Noticing the needs
I do my best to keep my integrity in help-
ing meet those needs
I allow myself to be adaptable while still keep-
ing congruent to who I am
It is a beautiful dance
Every single day I breathe
I breathe to remember who I am

DAY 26: BREATHING BREAKTHROUGHS

"WE CANNOT SOLVE OUR PROBLEMS WITH THE SAME THINKING WE USED WHEN WE CREATED THEM."
- ALBERT EINSTEIN

There is a famous quote by Albert Einstein, "We cannot solve our problems with the same thinking we used when we created them." I agree, and I also believe that when people hear that quote, they think about changing their thought process with the educated mind. However, the most efficient and effective way to shift perspective and how you think is to connect to Soul and/or Spirit. **My breakthrough this morning revealed that breathwork is one of our greatest assets for helping us connect to Spirit.**

Spiritual experiences are dependent upon altered states of consciousness. So, what is a Spiritual experience? It is when we tap into what many would call the unknown or the fourth dimension, that which goes beyond the typically perceived physical reality. I believe we all inherently know we are part of something much bigger than we commonly experience. And we are. According to scientific calculations by particle physicists, the known world (everything we can measure and aware of) only accounts for five percent of the Universe. The other 95 percent is called *dark matter* and *dark energy* (that which we can scientifically estimate exists, but currently do not have the technology to showcase it).

In another interesting conversation with Dr. Marvin Talsky the other day, he explained to me that in every language, there is a word for breath that relates to Spirit. In English, to "inspire" is to be "in-Spirit." For those who are wanting to embrace thinking differently and are looking for a breakthrough, breathwork is the key! It is the missing ingredient.

Too many people "think" they can "think" their way through. That is what I was doing. I was in a rut for several days. The social media thing was bugging me. I was trying to figure some things out for my company, and, what I really needed was to breathe! So I started the breaths, and new potentials emerged as I entered an altered state. It was in that altered state I got the information I needed, and then I started to move.

I'm not trying to tell you to abandon logic completely. You are still going to use your logic and your educated mind for discernment, strategy, planning, prioritization, and execution. Just know it is not the driver, it is not in control. **Give your Soul and Spirit the wheel, and follow through on their insight and guidance.**

I want you to start to notice this with me. In an elevated state, when you are breaking through the boundaries of this physical dimension, there is a "ping." There is a high-pitched sound that starts to take place. Almost like you have a ringing in your ears, but it is in the distance. It happens every time. It is also part of the Ayahuasca experience. You know you are in it deep when you start to hear the "ping." It happened today in the sauna during my breathwork, and breathwork is the most sustainable and natural way to enter this state.

The key—and what helped me to find the ping —is to imagine the breath continuing up into the center of the brain even after finishing breathing all the way in. So, you take your inhale to the point where you are filling the lungs to their maximal capacity, then visualize that inhale continuing even further. When you think about going more, even though you are not breathing more, you will track the breath going from the upper chest, through the throat, up the brainstem, and into the pineal gland. As you are thinking about all those spots filling up with air, you should start to feel a slight sensation of pressure in each of these areas. It can also feel like a wave of vibration flowing through your senses.

If you want to accentuate the feeling of the

wave, start your inhale in a flexed position, then allow yourself to lean slightly backward as you come to the end of your inhale. As you exhale, again return to a slightly flexed forward position. As you get rhythmic with this, a wave of influence will come over your body. You can also accomplish experiencing the wave purely with your breath. It just takes a bit more focus and presence.

Tony Robbins says, the difference between success and failure is a matter of two millimeters. A mere two millimeters can make all the difference. Even if you have done breathwork before, you just got one cue that can allow you to breathe much deeper into Spirit. It may be a "small" cue, but it can make all the difference.

ΔΔΔ

ACTIVITY

"Universal Breathing" Exercise: Three-Part Inhale

1. At the first part of your inhale (through the nose), focus on your diaphragm lowering into the abdominal cavity as your abdominal cavity expands in 360 degrees to increase space for this action.

2. The second part of your inhale has focus on the ribcage slightly elevating and also expanding in 360 degrees.

3. The third part of the inhale focuses on elevating

your clavicle (aka collarbone) to continue the expansion at the upper part of the lung space to complete a full inhale.
Eventually, you won't have to think about the inhale in three separate steps, but one complete action that engages all three areas.

"Universal Breathing" Exhale

On the exhale (through the mouth), don't allow all of the expansion you have created to collapse entirely. Create and maintain intra-abdominal pressure (pressure generated from inside of abdomen) by holding your body in a state of expanded tension.

To help visualize intra-abdominal pressure, think about what it feels like to palpate a dog's stomach. Dogs (and other four-legged horizontal animals) typically require an incredible amount of intra-abdominal pressure to stabilize and protect their internal organs. As humans, our vertical position to earth does not naturally require as much intra-abdominal pressure, but it is something we can train to help optimize our posture, breathing, and movements.

Breathwork Exercise

1. Complete five "Universal Breathing" cycles of: 11-count inhale, seven-count hold, 11-count exhale, seven-count hold.

2. When you start the hold, build a wave of that pressure that begins from the pelvis and then reaches up

to your brain and pineal gland.

3. After three seconds of the hold, start to increase the pressure with your attention and contraction of the muscles in your body. Aim to escalate the pressure of the breath hold continually, and at the count of seven, allow for a big release. By doing this, you will feel a rush of endorphins, energy, and blood flow.

You know you are being effective in the breathwork if your body is tingling. You know you are really effective if you hear the ping. If you didn't hear the ping, keep going. If you feel tension in a particular area of your body while doing this exercise, disperse the tension throughout your entire system and focus on bringing your attention and awareness back to the pineal gland. By performing this breathwork, you are activating the upper three chakras, assisting the body to find its ideal tension state, and reconnecting to Spirit. This is exactly where you want to be for transitioning into meditation. Always prep your meditation with breathwork, it makes it so much easier.

DAY 27: SPINAL CORD AS HARMONIZER

THE SPINAL CORD AS THE VIBRATORY HARMONIZER WITH GOD.

When talking about the nerve system, I like to imagine a floating brain with a spinal cord, which is basically a continuation of the brain. So you have the brain, this floating cord, and all of these little branches that leave the cord. This nerve system, that is floating in space, is how our body senses and perceives the world. It will regulate its tone—for itself, and how it communicates with the rest of the system—to best adapt to what is happening.

When stresses in life are too much for that nerve system to handle (overwhelm), it will distort and put itself in a state where it attempts to down-regulate the amount of information that is coming in and going out. Usually, there is a tightening or torsion of the cord based on how this stress comes into the system. In these moments, the nerve system and body will lock the stress in with a "snapshot" of the distortion. This snapshot is what I believe chiropractors are detecting as the spinal subluxation and misalignment. When our bodies are unable to adapt to incoming stress adequately, we distort and lock-in, creating stored potential energy.

There are two forms of energy: kinetic energy and potential energy. Kinetic energy is moving and dynamic. Potential energy is stored and static. If you think contraction, tightening, torsion, and then a snapshot; what is happening is this kinetic, dynamic energy, which is usually in flow with Universe, now becomes stored potential.

There is nothing good or bad about potential energy, it just is. It is a strategy of a living system not to let itself get completely burnt out with incoming energy or stress. All energetic systems have boundaries for what they can and cannot integrate. Let's use a circuit breaker for example. If there is a surge of energy that enters a circuit that is beyond the boundaries of that energetic system, the circuit breaker will kick in and stop that excess energy, limiting the amount of energy/information coming in, to avoid burning it all out.

Our body has a similar mechanism, the nerve system, which can contract, increase tension, and/or torsion, to transform kinetic energy into a snapshot of stored energy. Why is it stored? My theory is that the nerve system stores potential energy as a strategy for a potential future lesson. Stored energy is a stored memory of our INABILITY to adapt. It is a sign of where we need to evolve and get better. We "release" this stored potential when we fully acknowledge why it was created (the lesson). **I believe that our level of awakening has a relationship with our level of consciousness, awareness, and our energetic capacity to integrate information—aka, our adaptability**.

Adaptability is one of our greatest indicators of health. It is a direct reflection of our energetic integrative capacity. Inability to adapt to our environment creates distortion and dysfunction, which will create dis-ease, sickness, and disease over time. Our ability to adapt increases as our awareness increases. That is why it is so important to continuously reconnect to Spirit for a Universal perspective. Remember, **distortion and stored potential are lessons waiting to be learned**. To receive the lesson, you need to be open and **know that life is not happening to you, it's happening for you.** All of life's challenges can be considered blessings if you are willing to reveal the lesson.

Now that you understand the nerve system and how it regulates and monitors tone, and how it either adapts to stress or stores potential stress for future lessons, I want to shine another light. Visualize the nerve system as being an instrument with various cords. Imagine the peripheral nerves as strings coming off the spinal cord that go to every organ, muscle, tissue, and gland that we have—which means that if it stimulates the gland, it can regulate hormones. If it stimulates various tissue cells, it can create a tone that would be preferable or non-preferable for that tissue cell. If it goes to an organ, it can create specific contraction or expansion of that organ, which determines if it functions optimally or non-optimally. Same with muscles. The nerve stimulus will either generate a contraction or relaxation of the muscle that is coordinated or uncoordinated, functional or dysfunctional.

Think about how the pulse of electricity carries a vibration (imagine an echocardiogram). Within vibration is information. Information (stress) will either be adapted and integrated (kinetic) or locked-in and stored (potential). Incoming vibrations are sensed by our nerve system (brain, spinal cord, and peripheral nerves). If the nerve system is distorted, it is out of harmony with nature, and it's environment. The spinal cord is what you could say is our north star to the Universe. Our vibratory communicator with God/Spirit/Intelligence. When the tone of our cord is in Divine harmony, we begin to harmonize with ALL of life.

There are also three different meningeal layers of the spinal cord (dura mater, arachnoid mater, and pia mater), and each layer has its own vibratory mechanism. One layer is in resonance with the physical body, one layer at the level of the Soul, and one resonates with Spirit. Each with their distinct vibrancy of transmission. I believe the most subtle of these cord layers (pia mater) is in closest relationship with Spirit. Would be cool to see some studies generated on this in the future.

Most people are only noticing and experiencing life within their physical body. This means they are only tuning into the physical frequency. But there is more. Way more! Just think about the different colors that various animals can perceive. The smelling power of a dog, the listening of a dolphin, and the vision of an owl at night. And then, think about the inherent powers of the human that have been forgotten over time.

As we awaken in consciousness, we will begin to tap into more information within "the field" and become more sensitive to the vibration of our Soul and Spirit. I remember Lunar cycles and astrology used to mean jack shit to me. Now, I'll sense a pattern emerging in practice, and I will have a sense that the moon must be in a certain phase, or there must be meteor showers or some type of retrograde happening, and then I'll look it up, and find out I am 100 percent right, every time. If you can start notice trends on the physical, open yourself up to start to notice changes of the "subtle" Universe. When your awareness expands, it expands beyond your physical self.

DAY 28: NOTHING CHANGES IF NOTHING CHANGES

CONTINUOUSLY ASSOCIATING WITH PEOPLE WHO THINK AND VIEW THE WORLD AS YOU DO IS A PREDICTOR FOR STAGNANCY. PEER GROUPS OF VARIED PERSPECTIVE OFFER THE GREATEST OPPORTUNITY FOR CONTINUAL EVOLUTION (IF YOU CAN ADAPT).

In 2018, I experienced more growth than I have ever experienced in my life. One of the reasons for this is my willingness to associate with different opinions and perspectives. Another key is that these varied perspectives are coming from people who are doing really fucking well. It has been said in many ways, many times, "you become the people you spend the most time with." If you look around at the top five people around you, I guarantee you will be at a similar socioeconomic status, have a similar thought process, and resonant physicality, emotional well-being, and intelligence.

There are many similarities between you and who you associate with. So if you do not like who you are, take a look around your circle. Remember you are attracting the vibration you are, and that vibration is largely affected by the people that you are spending time with. When you change your peer group, you are also changing yourself, and by changing yourself, your peer group will also change. With that said, nothing changes if nothing changes. We often stay in groups that are comfortable even when we think we want to grow. It is convenient to seek people out who believe and perceive just like us. People who share the same ideals and the same philosophy on life bring comfort to our ego and identity.

Seeking and joining masterminds OUTSIDE my “sphere” is a strategy I utilize for overcoming the comfort of staying the same. I take a look at who has a specific skill-set, mindset, or perspective that I would like to learn, to adapt, and embrace. I look for masterminds that will help me with a topic or trait that is part of the next step of my evolution. By doing so, I am creating opportunities for my continual expansion. If I have a deep knowing that I really want to grow in marketing, I need to seek out a group who have the best mentors and coaches on marketing, regardless of whether they are in my industry or not. For example, chiropractors tend to want to learn only from other chiropractors, and this is a HUGE MISTAKE. Marketing "experts" within chiropractic are often mediocre at best when compared to some of the best marketers in the game. I did not learn this until I went outside my industry and was blown away by some of the wizards that exist out there in this world. Now, I get to leverage this new understanding in my own industry.

Recently I attended Tony Robbins *Business Mastery.* There were 3,000 people in attendance, and the average income per person was *over* one million dollars a year. Imagine what would shift in your perspective to share a room with 3,000 millionaires. Do you think new possibilities would open up? What would change within your vibrational potential? When you put yourself in incubators or masterminds that expose you to perspectives different from your own, especially in areas you would like to grow, the world opens up for you.

Adaptability is also something to keep in mind here. If you "overstretch" yourself, greater than 10-15 percent outside your comfort zone, and you cannot adapt, then there is no evolution. Remember, there is no process that does not require time. Know your value, know where you need to grow, and discover a tribe that will help take you there.

So, where are you stagnant? Where do you want to grow? Where do you need to *grow*? Start asking yourself the question, "where am I going to find the group with the education, the wisdom, and the opportunity to grow?" Continual evolution is a possibility. For anyone who is feeling stagnant in your life, you don't have to stay there! Continual evolution is in attunement with nature, with God, and with Source. We live in a Universe that is constantly expanding, and so are you. If you are not feeling that, then you are out of alignment. Let this be your wake up call to get aligned!

ΔΔΔ

ACTIVATION

It is not all on me
I find the space
In that space of the infinite
There are times when the busy mind feels like it is taking over
Like the stress is relentless
I find the space
I find my breath
And I am back
Back to the Universal SELF
The Universal SELF that knows all things
Is all powerful
It does not need a strategy

It just knows
And I am that
So I feel a great sense of calm and ease take over my system
I am feeling guided
I am feeling supported
I am feeling loved
I am love
I do not need to become love
I am love
Right here and right now
For I am Intelligence
And I am ready

DAY 29: WATER FAST

THE MIRACLE OF FASTING & ITS ABILITY TO BREAK PATTERN, DETOX-IFY, REGENERATE, & REVITALIZE.

Typically, I water fast once a week. Lately, with all my traveling, and the seven day fast I did not too long ago, I have been feeling a resistance to fast. I am currently in a strength building phase, and wanting to gain a bit of weight. I've done some short, intermittent fasts, but I haven't done a 24-hour water fast in at least a month. Finally, I was able to do a full day fast yesterday during one of my biggest service days in practice.

My busiest days are currently Mondays. My day begins at 5 a.m., I usually get into the office around 7 a.m., serve chiropractic until 12:30 p.m., then host meetings or shoot videos, then another chiropractic shift from 3-6:30 p.m., then "The Mandala experience" (a 1:1 healing experience that often goes into the spiritual realm) until 10 p.m.. That's a 17-hour day, and I love to do it in a fasted state.

Continuously, I have felt that fasting is one of the best ways to break free from my physical attachment and access more of my spiritual SELF. Historically, if you look at some of the messiahs, or avatars, or highly spiritual beings, you will see a trend of performing extended fasts. Jesus was said to have done a 40-day fast, Siddhartha/Buddha did a 40-day fast, Gandhi did a lot of fasting.

Fasting can also help us in the emotional realm. A lot of people are stuck in reactive mode. There is a difference between reacting and responding. With reactions, you often feel like you have very little control. Something happens, and based on your current survival strategies (that are heavily influenced by your past), you react in a way that could be an asset OR a liability in your life. When you respond, you create a space for observation of what you are experiencing. Then, YOU CHOOSE how you wish to respond. In response, you are way more likely to act from a place of inspiration and create more positive outcomes in your life.

I have definitely had a previous pattern of anger. And, it still shows up from time to time. Two years ago on Thanksgiving, I got into an actual fist fight with my brother. I had not had an act of violence in a few years. It is still in there ... and our families tend to know how to push our buttons in ways that bring out old traits of us. So, this is something I continue to work on. Something I am discovering now is that abnormal outward acts of anger or rage are often due to suppressed tears and sadness. My intention is that I continue to explore myself in ways that I can show up in the future with better responses.

There are also incredible physical benefits of fasting. My body has been feeling fatigued and the last few weeks have been very trying for me. I traveled to Vegas for five days, then came back for a day in the Bay, then I was off to Amsterdam to speak and teach, then Slovakia where I spent 14 hours getting tattooed over two days. Getting tattooed really taxes your immune system and nervous system, and I was already exhausted. Between that and all the traveling, I have been feeling my system get worn down. Typically, most would find it counterintuitive to NOT EAT when energy is feeling low. However, if you look at any animal in nature, when they are sick, they do not eat. They have an inborn instinct to fast in order to heal.

Think about how much metabolic energy is required for digestion. That is one of the primary things our bodies do regularly—up to 8-12 hours to digest a meal all the way through the cycle. For many of us, we are still attempting to digest food even while we are sleeping. When we fast, that energy can be transformed for healing and cellular repair. Autophagy is the cellular process that occurs with calorie restriction, which allows sick and dying cells to be replaced with healthy cells. It's a simple and essential cellular detoxification.

I have interacted with quite a people that

think fasting is not for them because they do not "feel good" when doing it. There is a reason for that. **The sicker and more toxic your body is, the harder the fast will be.** That is because of the natural detoxification process. When your body is trying to purge toxic shit, it will not feel great when you are getting rid of it. Your body will detoxify through the skin, liver, kidneys, and bowel. And yes, it can be uncomfortable, but the more you lean into fasting as a habit for vitality, the more it will be an ally in your ideal life expression.

One of my first water fasts was a seven-day fast. The night before I started, I went out for Mexican food with friends and had a few shots of tequila to wash down my big ass burrito. I had never done an extended fast before and somehow decided it would be a "good idea" to go for seven days to test my willpower (ego). I felt like shit. Like I got ran the fuck over. Starting on day three, I developed a huge rash on my back near my kidneys. On the fifth day, I developed nyctalopia (night blindness) in my left eye and still kept going. I was getting hypoglycemic shakes, feeling like my skin was crawling and could not sleep. On day six, it was hard for me to have the energy to walk. I went through all this while still a full-time chiropractic student and adjusting people at the health center. I distinctly remember almost passing out three separate times from interacting with patients and then needing to lay down for 30 minutes trembling with low blood sugar. What I was experiencing was my body purging all the toxicity I had been exposed to or consumed in my past. It was not pretty or preferred, but I made it through.

Now, I have learned there are far more optimal ways to enter a fast. You can start your fast a week prior with a low-carb diet to help prep the body for Ketosis and get you used to burning fat for fuel instead of carbohydrates. Also, having a bit of sea salt during your fast will help maintain essential minerals and avoid dehydration headaches. A 24-hour fast is the safest for beginners. Three days or more is advanced. For those interested, after I finished my fourth seven-day water fast, I shot a masterclass video on this that can be found on my Dr. Brett Jones Facebook page. Remember, when fasts are performed safely, on the other side of the discomfort is vitality, clarity, and a greater connection to Soul and Spirit.

ΔΔΔ

ACTIVATION

At this moment I am grateful for the slowdowns
As much as I am grateful for the speed and the intensity
I am grateful for savoring
Savoring the victories and the love
Savoring the connections
I savor the moments
I am grateful for the simple things today

I am grateful to have coffee again this morning
I am grateful for hugs
I am grateful for a roof over my head
I am grateful for a warm bed to sleep in
I am grateful for amazingly refreshing clean drinking water
I am grateful for my opportunities and my blessings
And I am grateful for my challenges
Knowing that if I am receiving new challenges, it is a sign of growth
I am grateful
Thank you, thank you, thank you

DAY 30: ACCOUNTABILITY THROUGH TEACHING

INCREASING ACCOUNTABILITY & IMPACT WITH TEACHING & FACILITATING.

Teaching and facilitating learning for others has a massive potential to increase your level of accountability, impact with your community, and contribution to humanity. I can directly attribute a lot of my personal success in business and in chiropractic from my willingness to enter teaching and leadership positions. Every time I *schedule* a new workshop, retreat, training camp, seminar, or online webinar, I am committing to level up and show up better than I was before.

One of the reasons things never get done in our life—that book we want to write, that podcast we want to start, or that workshop we want to create—is because it never gets scheduled. Everything that has been created in my life is because I have scheduled a "startline" for it. Some people like to call it a deadline, I like to call it startline. If I am creating from Soul connection, I *start* to increase my quality of LIFE. So, set a date, schedule it as a startline, and declare it to your friends and community. Know that your integrity is on the line if you don't follow through. Set a startline, even if you do not know how it is going to get done. One of the best questions you can ask is, "if it could be done, how would it be done?" **The Universe will organize in your favor when you seek possibilities instead of limitations.** Know that if you are called to do big things, a lot of times people are going to tell you, "That will never work! That's not possible!" And they are right. It will never work, and it's not possible ... FOR THEM. But you ain't like them! You eat challenges for breakfast and shit excellence. *You Know Who the Fuck You Are.*

So far, some of my biggest lessons in accountability and the art of facilitation are from being a Lead Facilitator with Kairos Training Culture. At our training camps, our Lead Facilitators are required to go ALL-IN. We are not just telling you what to do, we are right there in the trenches with you, TRAINING! By requiring all of our facilitators to fully participate, we are creating a high level of accountability because no one wants to show up out of shape and get their asses handed to them by the people they are supposed to be training.

Another example of how I leveraged the responsibility of teaching for personal accountability is with the creation of this group (*The Unshakeables*). Monday through Thursday I am committed to doing a video at 6 a.m., which holds me accountable for waking up by 5:15 a.m. to complete my movement, breathwork, and meditation before I go live. I am way more committed to a morning ritual when I know people are depending on me to show up for them clear and connected. I do not want my messages to come from the mental realm, I want them to come from another dimension, and to do tha takes preparation.

By knowing the voice of our Soul and following guidance from Spirit, we stay in alignment with our Unshakeable Purpose. When you are clear, you will find yourself communicating things that are not coming from an educated mind. It means you are not re-creating or duplicating anything. You are actually *creating*. You are directly helping this world 's consciousness to evolve. What a beauty that is, that you are contributing, not just to the people who are learning, but to humanity. You are contributing to all sentient beings because you are bringing something forth that had never been brought forth before. That is how things shift, that is how we awaken.

ΔΔΔ

ACTIVATION

Whatever feelings of uncertainty and weak-
ness that are lingering in my system
Telling me that I am not enough
Just let it go
Maybe they are telling me I am too much
Because that can be the case sometimes too
No matter where I am at
No matter who I feel I am
In this moment, I am all that I need to be
I am continuously revealing the depths of who I am
Today I walk and I talk with just a little bit more certainty
A little bit more collective power
A little bit more humility
A little bit more vulnerability
A little bit more integrity
A little bit more strength
A LOT more love
I am excited for the continual growth and
evolution that is happening
For self and for the bigness of SELF
The world around me is organizing for me based on
my level of consciousness and awareness
Any suffering that I may perceive is a misperception
I move forward in redirecting the percep-

tion to be an asset in my life

To be empowering in my life

I am seeking new opportunities to reprogram the mind

To be in full integrity with the universal I Am

I am ready

I am happy

I am fulfilled

DAY 31: BREATHWORK & VISUALIZATION FOR CONNECTION, GRATITUDE, & LOVE

10-MINUTE BREATHWORK & VISUALIZATION FLOW FOR CONNECTION, GRATITUDE, & LOVE.

Find a place where you are seated comfortably with your ears stacked over your shoulders, your shoulders stacked over your hips, your chest is lifted.

As you start taking breaths, inhale through the nose for seven counts, hold for three, exhale for seven through the mouth, hold for three, and then inhale for seven again.

Repeat this three times.

Keep going through these cycles with this cadence while going through the following cueing:

Now we are going to micro-tune this system as we go through the breathing.

As we go through this, I want you to think about where some of your joints may feel compressed.

As you breathe, imagine you are filling those spaces with air.

Almost like there is an airbag that is being filled, and it is creating space.

As it creates space, you feel freedom in the joints.

You feel freedom in the spine.

It feels as though it is starting to float in space and your system is getting lighter.

As you exhale, keep that space.

Notice what you need to do, with just a slight movement with the head, either back in extension, forward in flexion, or in rotation, or in bringing your shoulders down, or slightly rotating a hip or knee.

Just look for your body to take out all of its tensional and compressional points so that you feel free in your system and you are doing it through breath.

Continue the cadence.
With every inhale feeling lighter and lighter, feeling more space.

Now we are going to bring our awareness—

as we continue the breathing—to where we feel pressure when we think a thought.

Most people's conscious mind projects two to three inches in front of their forehead.

When we are thinking about where we are at in space, it is usually forward projecting, and very rarely backward projecting.

Right now, bring that thought back into the center of your head.

Now, with your eyes closed, bring your awareness, first to right in front of the eyelids to the skin.

How does the skin react with your environment?

Feel the slight temperature difference between your body and the external environment.

Now go behind the eyelids.

As you do this, you should see a shift in color.

Now there is blood vasculature, often people will see more reds and yellows as they bring their awareness behind the eyelid.

Start to feel just a little bit of pressure not only into the eyelid but also the eyeball. Again, the colors will change and shift.

Now focus on using your eye strength to now pull the eyeballs back into the socket.

You should feel pressure now behind your eyeball.

Continue the breath cycle—inhale through the nose for seven, hold for three, exhale through the mouth for seven, hold for three.

Now you are feeling a little bit of pressure behind the eyeball.

Hold that pressure and see what that feels like.

On the next inhale, continue to hold that pressure but also continue to float your entire system in space.

Feel yourself becoming lighter and lighter and lighter.

More connected to the Universe.

Less connected to the compressional sites of the physical body.

Now sink your awareness from the eyeball to the socket.

Now you are pulling back your thoughts, and your conscious mind and your attention is now going into the bony area of your skull, and you should feel a change of substance.

Instead of thinking fleshy, eyeball tissue, now you are going into the density of the skull which also has its own energy.

Pull back even further.

Now you are getting into the outer layer of the brain, the meninges that wrap and how they are connected to your spinal cord, which goes all the way down to the sacrum.

There is this flow and channel of life as you hit that outer meningeal layer, and as your awareness is right on front of the brain at the back of the eye socket you are connected first to the meningeal system, and you are recognizing it with your breath.

As you are breathing, you are noticing how your breath creates some spinal movement, and there is also this pumping of cerebrospinal fluid which is carried through the depths of the meninges that are not just bathing the spinal cord but also the brain.

Now pull your awareness back a little bit further.

Now we are getting into the brain tissue and depending on your sensitivity you may start to feel some of the electrical conductivity.

We know that we are electrical, energetic beings and a lot of that is carried within our brain and within our spinal cord and peripheral nerves.

Now we are pulling back into the actual brain.

Keep going. Go even further.

Now focus.

If you had to draw a line through your temples and they met someplace in the middle, you are getting closer to the pituitary and pineal gland.

Let's focus on the pineal gland.

As you focus on the center and towards the pineal gland, think about how can you use your system and intention and awareness to retract all of the tissue and thought into that one area.

Still breathing—seven, three, seven, three.

Now think about one specific thought in the center of the brain, where all the intention and awareness is going.

As you start to focus on the pineal gland, this is where you can see the burst of colors, the kaleidoscope or universal geometry.

Just breathing there. Relaxed, with comfort.

Continuing the breathing cycle.

Now, in this space of connection, we want to send universal wisdom ... we want to feel that connection.

With your inhale, feel as though you are gathering even more of this energy that is all around us.

As you inhale you feel filled up with light radiant energy and that energy is healing your system. It is sometimes golden light, or indigo blue, or white light.

For now, you are in that dark space in the pineal gland, that is connected to all, and you are collecting energy with every inhale.

With every exhale you are letting it go in return

to the Universe, knowing that it is abundant.
Inhale, collecting all the energy around you,
soothing and healing your body.

Exhale, returning.

There is a continuous cycle.

You are being filled up more and more and more with your awareness in this torus of connection that is constantly inflowing and outflowing with ease.

Continue your breath cycle of seven, three, seven, three.

We are going to bring our awareness to gratitude for everything we have at this moment.

Being fully grateful. Knowing that the more we are grateful for what we've got, the more we will get to be grateful for.

Often it is an image that will pop up and often it is a smile that will go across the face, and a feeling of warmth and your throat opens up, and your eyes might even start to well up just a little bit, especially if you can find that deep gratitude for everything that you are today. Not everything that you need to be, but everything that you are and for all that already surrounds you.

Just a reminder that there is always so much to be grateful for and in that gratitude we can get connected even more to the present.

Keep cycling with this gratitude for another 30 seconds. Really feel one concept or image and move on to an-

other but continue your breathing. Gratitude.

From gratitude, we will move into love.

Love is the intelligence of this Universe. It is what organizes energy and matter. Love is always there, sometimes we just don't take the time to feel it.

At this moment we are revealing more love that is us and surrounds us. Knowing that we don't need to become love or be loved. We are love.

We are a more loving being today than we were yesterday.

As people meet and greet us, they step into a love bubble.

They realize that they now have more love for themselves and others.

WE are a constant revealer of love for the self and the depths of the big SELF that is ALL.

Just like that energy that was entering the system in abundance, so is love.

Love is ALL.

We cannot run dry on love.

We cannot outgive love. When it is love, it is always there.

DAY 32: SHOCK OF PRESENCE

BREAK UNCONSCIOUS PATTERNS TO REACH NEW LEVELS OF AWARENESS

This ties into the previous lesson on the 10 percent variety, 90 percent consistency for health. I had the opportunity to go to bed early last night. I put my boy down around 8:30 p.m. and ended up passing out with him. Usually, I set my alarm for 5 a.m. and get up around 5:15. Since I went to bed early, I set my alarm for 4:30 a.m.. That allowed me to go into 30+ minutes of movement and breathwork and 25 minutes of meditation and sauna. I even had the opportunity to shower before getting on the call this morning. This simple change-up in routine allowed me to shock the system.

In both the physical and psychological aspects, it is important to discover what your normal threshold is, then create opportunities to push through it. We need variety and challenge so that we do not become stagnant, compressed, and close-minded. Even though I have been doing my morning routine, it has been the same thing or similar for the past seven weeks. So, today I found room to take my breathing and meditation to the next level, and it was incredible!

When we go outside our ordinary routine and shock the system, we shock it into presence. After a while, if your routine is too similar, you will begin to develop unconscious competence, which means you can perform actions without having to think about them. This evolution in learning has the ability to make you efficient; however, it can also lead to you being very distracted. For example, when you first started driving a car, you thought about every little detail (blinker on three seconds in advance to signify you were changing lanes, looking over your shoulder, using your mirrors, etc.) Now, you could be driving a car, sending a text message, turning the radio station, and yelling at your kid in the backseat, all at the same time. In this example, unconscious competence does not guarantee you to be a better driver. Without focus, the quality of performance decreases. Presence with Spirit and Soul is the goal.

If you find yourself going through the motions, how can you embrace diversity in your life to create challenges to shock the system? If you have been doing 10-20 minute meditations, what would it look like if you did an hour? If you have been doing two rounds of breath work, what does it look like if you do five? If you have been running a mile what does it look like when you run six? You have got to test the system. In these acute stress moments, if the system adapts to it, there is massive evolution. In physiology, this positive health adaptation to low dose stress is called hormesis. You do not need to destroy yourself, just look for the opportunities to push your boundaries.

A common misperception is that you need to be in peak physical state to to challenge yourself. This is actually the opposite of the truth. Overcoming fears and challenges are how you get optimal health. Think about this, some people live their entire lives never feeling ready to push themselves. I call them the "tomorrow people." Tomorrow I will get started with that workout. Tomorrow I will begin my diet. Tomorrow I will get that paper done. Tomorrow I will make that phone call. Tomorrow, tomorrow, tomorrow... And guess what?! Tomorrow may never come. I learned this the hard way with the death of my brother. So, NOW seems like a good time to start. If you don't feel ready, try failing. Then fail harder. Failure only stays a failure if you never attempt to succeed again.

ΔΔΔ

ACTIVITY

Challenge yourself to shock your system in one way

or another this week. If you are used to doing cold water immersion, you need to go colder or longer. If you are used to doing breath holds, you need to go longer or do more repetitions. If you are used to doing meditations, I challenge you to sit for three times longer than you are used to sitting. If you are doing a lot of movement or exercise, I challenge you to shock the system.

ΔΔΔ

ACTIVATION

Thank you Source for the opportunities
To continually get better
To continually dive in so that I can be and express my best self
Thank you for the reminders
Thank you for the reconnections
Thank you for the consciousness, awareness, and energetic capacity that is growing day by day
Thank you for my ability to adapt to internal and external environments
Thank you for my ability to love and understand what love is
Thank you for my ability to acknowledge that I am wrong sometimes as well

But by being wrong, I have an opportunity to
realize my mistakes and make further adap-
tations for continual evolution
Thank you for allowing me to be in circles
that encourage me to get better
Knowing that it matters
It matters that I am my best self
So I am committed to the journey
It excites me
It enlivens me!
I am exhilarated by it, not defeated by it
Bring on the challenges
Bring on the growth
I am here, and I am ready

DAY 33: RECUPERATION MEDITATION

Find a space where you can be seated in
a comfortable position
Stack the ears over the shoulders, the shoul-
ders over the hips
Begin to quiet both the outside and inside, both
the external and internal environments
Slowly removing the stimulus
Find your breath as a silver lining…
That one piece of connection to Spirit
See how thin that strand is
Remove everything that is not
You can remove it by floating it
As you inhale, imagine your system getting a lit-
tle bit lighter, and a little bit more free
There is more space in the stillness
With every breath, going deeper into the void,

deeper into the black space
Deeper into the vortex
In this space, there is no need to be anything
There is no need to be anywhere
There is no need to think
There is no need to strategize
It just is
And you just are
In this black space
In this void, this vortex
Know that you are deeply supported
Know that you are deeply loved
Know that you are deeply held
Know that you are being healed
Healing is recognizing your wholeness
To recognize your wholeness, you just need to be
So, again, remove everything that you are not
Find that space
That stillness
The void
The vortex
Breath into that
It is getting quieter and quieter
Stiller and stiller

One strand connected to Spirit
No need to do anything
No need to think
Finding the still space
Finding the void
Entering the vortex
Just breathing
We are healed when we recognize our wholeness
We recognize our wholeness when we just be
Remove everything that is not
Find the stillness
Enter the black space
Enter the void
Enter the vortex
You are whole
You are loved
You are here
You are now

DAY 34: GRATITUDE FOR HOLDING SPACE

GRATITUDE & ACKNOWLEDGEMENT FOR THOSE THAT HOLD SPACE FOR US.

We would not be who we are right here in this moment without those who continuously hold space for us in very unique ways. Sometimes it feels like direct support. Sometimes their beingness of creating space is allowing us to express in the way that we do. Sometimes, even those that we believe are criticizing us, or challenging us, are also contributing to creating the space that is needed for us to be who we be.

Alan Watts has a quote, "I am not I if you are not you, and you are not you if I am not I." **The only way we understand self is in relation to others, especially in this physical dimension.** For those that appear different or opposite to us, their beingness is allowing us to be who we are in response and reflection. It is essential to take the time to acknowledge those that are continuously holding space for us.

I spent most of yesterday morning in a recuperative state. Anytime that I started to think that I needed to do something, I relinquished it and allowed myself just to be. There will be time for all the doing, I had to just be. I was only able to be in this recuperative state because I have support. The people I needed to step in and help out, came to my aid and got shit done.

We have talked about adaptability, levels of consciousness, and awareness. I believe they are all inter-related. As of late, I have had many stressful challenges come my way. At this time, based on my current level of adaptability, I could not handle it. Straight up. There was a lot. Many people in similar situations end up pushing until they have a nervous breakdown. For me, I knew I needed to downregulate the information and stress coming in, and to do that, I needed to relinquish my worry about all the things that need to be done. That was my strategy yesterday, to create space for myself to heal.

That healing allowed me to return to The Source Chiropractic in a completely refreshed state. I felt rejuvenated, and it is the best my body has felt in the last month or so. I am grateful for the listening and awareness, and grateful to be able to relinquish the "producer" in me that is always doing the most.

ΔΔΔ

ACTIVITY

Think about the people in your life who you are in close proximity with. Those who you interact with on a daily basis. Notice how their action or non-action has been continuing to allow how you express in this world. We are who we are in this moment as a reflection of those who hold space for us. So, be grateful.

Then start to think about your family and those you are in close direct relationship with. Start with siblings and parents. Whatever the relationship is today, acknowledge through action or non-action, the space that has been created for you is a direct reflection of how you are expressing in this world. Remove the good or bad label, for they are relative, and just notice what you notice.

After that, go to the extended family: cousins, uncles, aunts. Still part of your bloodline and ancestry. How do they hold space for you to be who you be? Expand to friends. Maybe even ones we do not interact with daily but people in our life that have helped shape us. We may not even talk to them anymore, but there is a space there. That space is constantly funneling our expression. We are grateful for exactly who we are today.

Finally, expand to acquaintances. Those who have entered our life and maybe not stayed a part of our life but have made an impact. Every time that occurs, there is still space held, as distant as it may be. As you continue to go through this process, realize that every single being on this planet is crafting who we are. There is a tensegrity system of the entire Universe that we are a part of—not separate from—but entangled with, and exactly who we are is because of the ALL. I will take it a step further, you are the ALL.

An exercise like this allows us to step outside of the ego for a moment and realize that how we are expressing in this world is in direct relationship with how everyone else is expressing in this world. So, we show up. We listen. We find the needs and fill them. We value our needs as much as the needs of others. We are the whole, and the whole is us. We are the ALL, and the ALL is us. We are the infinite, and the infinite is us.

Exactly who you are expressing right here and right now is a reflection of those who hold space for you. Share appreciation, acknowledgment, love, trust and gratitude for exactly who you are, and who you are becoming, and all those who have shaped that expression in your life. For you are that and they are you.

DAY 35: THREE POWERFUL PHRASES

THE THREE MOST POWERFUL PHASES OF TRANSFORMATION & HEALING: I LOVE YOU, I FORGIVE YOU, & I AM SORRY.

Today's lesson is about the three most transformational and healing phrases that I know: I love you, I forgive you, and I am sorry. These three phrases can interrupt dysfunctional patterns and create an opportunity for empowering relationships. As I continue to deepen my understanding of these phrases, I gain more reverence for their utility in our lives.

During my recent meditation and breathwork sessions in the sauna, I have been imagining all of my BEing being cleared, healed, and reconnected to Spirit. I believe we experience disease, dysfunction, and disconnection due to misperception. The misperception that we are not already whole. The misperception that we are a body that has a Soul instead of a Soul that has a body. Reconnecting is feeling healed and whole at all levels. The next piece is getting into gratitude, feeling grateful for everything that you have and seeing how so many things in your life had to come into divine order for you to be exactly where you are.

As consciousness continues to awaken and evolve you realize that everything in your life is preparing you, molding you for who you need to become. The challenges and pain are lessons. **The more you understand that everything that enters your life is providing a lesson to prepare you for who you are becoming, the easier it is to become continuously grateful.**

From gratitude, it is about moving into physiological states associated with being the person that we are becoming and accomplishing the things we want to achieve. Ultimately, it is not the milestone, it is not the diploma, certification, or license. It is not the house. It is not the car. It is not the money. It is all about how are you going to *feel* and who are you going to *be*. By accomplishing this or that, who are you becoming? And what states of emotion do you get to experience?

The more you can go into those states, the more you are BEING, the more you will attract and manifest. We do not attract what we want, we attract what we are. Why not just be that now? If you assume you will feel a certain way once you make a certain amount of money, why not just be that now? If more stability and security will give you more certainty, which will allow you to feel powerful and make quick decisions, why not be that now? Even if it is just in visualization. The more you allow yourself to enter those states now, the more this Universe will start to reorganize in your favor.

Back to the three phases. We can use gratitude and presence to discover which of the three phrases is necessary for our healing. I like to start with visualizations of my family. Willow Moon flashes in with that big smile and the joy she brings into my life. I am so grateful for her. Then Jax and all he brings into my life. My wife, her loving support and co-leadership. And I start to think about my dad, my brothers, and then mom ... and as much as I feel like I have worked on it, it still seems like there is something unresolved when it comes to my mom. The tone of my thoughts shifted, and that is an indicator something is there. Now, I begin to go through the three phrases to find which one is the priority.

"I'm sorry."
"I forgive you."
"I love you."

As I'm saying "I love you," my voice cracked.

A change in pitch or vibration, a change in energy expression, or a change in physiology are all indicators for what needs healing. You will notice it when saying the three phrases, and when you do, that is what you need to lean into. A lot of us find these things as signs of weakness, but if we can discover them and move through them, they are actually our superpower. **Our ability to be vulnerable, and our ability to go ALL-IN, is how we grow, evolve, and heal.**

So, while visualizing my mom, I continue to say "I love you" again and again. Eventually, I feel sadness, and the sadness turns into tears. Since my brother passed we have had a very distant relationship, with many ups and downs, and in the last two years a big lack of communication. She has never met her granddaughter and only seen my boy twice. I believe the sadness that emerged is me missing her, and wishing she could be a bigger part of my life. This acknowledgment alone allowed me more insight on why I was feeling what I was feeling, started another healing process, and I was finally able to say "I love you" without a break in tone.

As you go through exercises like this and notice there is stuff there, do not be ashamed. Be excited, be curious, be intrigued, and then explore. I guarantee you will be a better expression of yourself by working through your dissonant tones.

ΔΔΔ

ACTIVITY

"I love you." "I forgive you." "I'm sorry." As you go through these three phrases, are there any relationships that come up in your life that need acknowledgment and healing? What phrase causes the most dissonance? Continue to say it until you receive the lesson and have cleared the field.

You do not have to actually say this phrase to the person unless you feel called to. The goal is to clear it within your own energetic field. Sometimes this requires breathwork, adjustments, fasts, screaming, or crying. Smetimes, it just moves to a different kind of charge, when you realize by saying "I love you" over and over, it really means "I miss you."

DAY 36: LIVING IN-SPIRIT

WHEN ONE IS IN-SPIRIT, THE RESOURCES THEY NEED WILL BE PROVIDED. LIVING IN-SPIRIT IS THE ULTIMATE RESOURCEFULNESS.

I am currently in Taiwan on a layover headed to Bali. Just finished a 13-hour flight beginning at 1:45 a.m., taking off from San Francisco. Based on our flight trajectory, it was "night" the entire time, beautifully dark.

It seems that there has been a significant amount of serendipity and divine arrangements in my life lately. It has been very interesting to observe it all playing out. For example, I just launched a new project with a colleague of mine, and we have been recruiting chiropractors that represent different aspects and expressions of success. One person I have really been wanting to bring in is Dr. Katina Manning. These past two weeks I have not been able to reach her because she has been traveling through Germany and Armenia on service trips. My business partner reminded me that everyone we have brought in so far has been provided by Source with ease and in flow, so when the timing is right, it will work out the way it is supposed to.

Last week when I picked up my wife from the airport, we had a coffee date before we went home to reunite with the kids. On our way home, she wanted to play a song for me that she had heard over the weekend that made her think of me. As Florence and the Machine's *Cosmic Love* played over the speakers, I immediately recognized the song because I used a different version of it for a video I produced to showcase Dr. Katina's chiropractic mastery. As I go to play the other version for my wife, I'm ten seconds into the song, and Katina calls. Synchronicities like this have been happening to me daily. Not just once and awhile, but every day. Like you think of someone, and there they are.

The last six weeks of my life have never moved so fast. For those that know me, that's saying a lot because I typically move pretty damn quickly. This new level of expansion has really tested my capacity. Yesterday, it took a lot for me to get into a state where I felt like I could be in service. I have had a lack of sleep and feel like I am moving into physical, mental, emotional, and spiritual exhaustion.

Then I got this flight that is supposed to be 13

hours. I upgraded to the next level, premium economy. I did not know what that meant or if I was going to be able to sleep. I'm 6'4", I did not know if I would have enough legroom. Once I get in, I see these are the best seats I have ever had in my life! Full reclining, plenty of room, and the headpiece hit me just right. So I put on my headphones and played some dreamtime binaural beats, and it was the best sleep I have had in three weeks! I knew that if I did not get that sleep, things would not be so good for me.

At that last moment, in the final hour, Source provided again. I believe that these things are being offered for me the way they are right now because I am more connected to Spirit than I have ever been. **If you are living inspired, you are living In-Spirit, and that is realizing you are One with the Infinite Intelligence.**

Our needs are provided when we remove what we are not and step into what we are. We will realize more of who we are when we expand our senses and tap into our psychic abilities, intuition, instinct, and insight. That is the beauty of living In-Spirit.

Who do you look up to for achieving what they achieved? For me, it is almost incomprehensible the things that BJ Palmer and Sid Williams were able to accomplish. BJ took over the Palmer School of Chiropractic when he was 19 years old! He wrote 39 volumes of books, had a printing press, radio station, traveled the globe, had the largest spinal specimen collection in the world, and revolutionized health as we know it. It is almost unfathomable until you realize that it is a story of a person living In-Spirit.

When you are In-Spirit, that is the ultimate resourcefulness because resources are not limited, they are as abundant and infinite as Source. When we know that we are the re-organizing Universe—that which attracts, manifests, and creates—we will be provided the resources and opportunities needed for us to evolve and heal.

This last weekend, my wife was away on tour at various chiropractic colleges for a project called "Rise Up Roadshow." I talked to her in the beginning, and she was super high energy and excited to meet up with all the students. I spoke to her Saturday night after she finished and her energy had shifted. She was going deep with people, so a lot of them were very emotionally connected to her and vulnerable with her. She felt it all and was experiencing a spiritual and emotional hangover. What a blessing! The reason I say that is few will ever be able to experience that.

I have experienced complete adrenal burn out once in my life, and it happened during my second quarter of chiropractic school. I was training intensely three hours per day for an MMA fight, was enrolled in 29 units at school, and had a long-distance girlfriend (now, my wife) and we were up late talking on the phone every evening. I was averaging maybe four hours of sleep every night. Again, what a blessing.

You may be thinking, "this guy is a masochist" but I say "what a blessing" because how many of us have actually pushed ourselves to see what failure looks like? To see what the limits are? I mean yes, there are more sustainable ways to do this, but every once in a while ... Shit, see what you've got! How far can you go emotionally? How much can you express vulnerability? How far can you go spiritually? How far can you explore physically? How deep does your training go?

I honestly believe most of us stay within 50 percent of what we are capable of because we are trying to sustain it. Yes, this can be a strategy. But other times, I am telling you right now, it is going to take a little bit more. What I am having to do right now, I do not suggest it as a long-term habit, but it is necessary for what Spirit is calling forth from me at this moment. The blessing is I am able to see how far my training goes, and where I'm falling short.

DAY 37: HONORING CREATIVITY CYCLES

TO CREATE SOMETHING NEW, WE HAVE TO GO OUTSIDE CURRENT FRAMES OF CONSCIOUSNESS.

As a creative person, understanding flows within the creative cycle are very important. Typically, we try to force creativity. We are wanting to get into a creative space, and we put a lot of pressure on ourselves, and that pressure is exactly what will diminish our ability to create and be in the flow. Ina May has a book about natural childbirth that talks about the "sphincter rule." When in labor, it's better to focus on relaxation and allowing the birth to happen instead of trying to force it or "push" through it. Similar to having a bowel movement. If you are struggling to take a shit, do not just push harder, you will hurt yourself and strain your butthole. Just relax and let that shit flow. Literally.

It is the same thing with the creative cycle. There are daily, weekly, monthly, and annual creative cycles. Meaning there may be certain times of the day, week, month, and/or year that you are more naturally creative. It is your job to discover these natural cycles, and when in resonance, that which you are trying to create will manifest with a higher frequency of success.

For instance, I prefer certain creative activities during certain times of the day. For delivering Spiritual messages, I prefer early mornings or late at night. I love these times because they are easier for me to get the educated mind out of the way and allow Universe to express through me. I am usually doing my morning ritual by 5 a.m. which includes breathwork, movement, meditation, and creative flows. Similarly, I find that I have better spiritual connectedness late at night, especially after a long day of service. When the body is physically exhausted, there is an excellent opportunity to drop-in with Spirit.

Once you have mastered your internal space and learn your own unique cycles of creative flow, changing your external environment can also spark different expressions of creativity. Whether that is going on a nature walk, biking an urban area, or swimming in a lake, environmental factors will alter the vibration of the incoming information. So, where is a space or place that you feel clear? Where is inspiring? What question do you have, and where would you go for the answer from Spirit?

Remember, for creation to happen, for us to create something new and not duplicate or repeat, we have to go outside the current frame of consciousness. These altered states will pull us out of the third-dimensional physical reality, and it is there, in the other, the ether, that we join the creative powers of the Universe.

ΔΔΔ

ACTIVATION

Feeling grateful for health

Feeling grateful to have an opportunity today to express

With all the abundance and all the love that I am

To find new ways and opportunities to con-

nect from the depths within

And from that internal connection

That it is expressed to all of those that are in

my vicinity and in my proximity

That they can feel the love, the connection, the

presence, the peace, the clarity

And by being in a field of that, they can become

that, they sense that, they move with that

Ultimately my being is the activator

I do not have to say anything

I do not have to do anything

That I keep strengthening my vibration
Through that vibration, change and
shift and evolution ...
And awareness and consciousness all evolve
I am excited about the opportunity to showcase the work
I am excited to continue the training
Every day I am better and better

DAY 38: THE POWER OF SELF-IMAGE

IT IS POSSIBLE TO BE VERY CERTAIN WITH DISEMPOWERING BELIEF SYSTEMS, WHICH CAN GIVE US FALSE PROJECTIONS OF SELF & OF OUR PARADIGM/PERSPECTIVE.

These passages from Psycho-Cybernetics are crucial. They are getting me to re-evaluate "self" in a different way. I have been a person who has done a lot of affirmations, or what some would call incantations. I have been a person that has built self and connected to self at higher levels continuously.

> "Positive thinking cannot be used effectively as a patch or crutch to the same old self-image. In fact, it is literally impossible to really think positively about a particular situation, as long as you hold a nega-

> tive concept of self. And, numerous experiments have shown that once the concept of self is changed, other things consistent with the concept of self, are accomplished easily without the strain."

> "Prescot Lecky conceived of the personality as a 'system of ideas,' all which must seem to be consistent with each other. Ideas which are inconsistent with the system are rejected, 'not believed,' and not acted upon. Ideas which seem to be consistent with the system of ideas—the keystone—the base upon which all else is built, is the individual's 'ego ideal,' his 'self-image,' or his conception of self."

One of the things that I have talked a lot about is the image and how important the image is for shaping our reality. However, I usually talk about the image as a projection of reality, or an altered reality, that we are stepping into. Using "image" as interchangeable with "vision" for self and what it is that you are trying to create. The stronger the image, the more likely you are to create it.

When I first started training in chiropractic, I set my intentions on being one of the best chiropractors in the world. While in chiropractic school, I interviewed masters in the field to discover the elements of an artful and successful chiropractor. I then transformed those elements into an image, and I have been chasing that image every day of my life for the last eight years. I figured If I am going to do this, and put my life into this, then I want to be the best that I can be. A sign of me becoming one of the best in the world would be people willing to travel far distances to come and receive an adjustment from me. That is starting to happen. Yesterday, all in one day, three separate people, one from

New York, one from Atlanta, and one from LA, all flew into Oakland, CA to receive an adjustment at The Source Chiropractic. That is the power of what is possible when you craft a sharp image, keep the focus, and are willing to do the work.

There is another aspect to the image, the self-image. Our world and the things that we accept as ideas, belief systems, paradigms, and programs, are centered continuously around our concept of self. Our idea of self is heavily influenced by our external environment. How many times can you hear something about the small self (the ego/personality) before at the very least subconsciously you start to believe that about yourself? By doing so, you are attracting and/or rejecting potential life outcomes every single day.

For example, I have had this disempowering belief (or self-image) that ultimately older males in the chiropractic profession had something against me, and that is why I am not getting levels of accolades, recognition, or invitations to speak on various stages. I thought, "there is something against younger males on the come up in the profession, that they often get neglected." Whether or not this is true, is this a disempowering or empowering belief? If I choose to continue thinking this way, the laws of attraction will keep creating a reality for me that supports my beliefs.

This is another fucking great lesson. **Many people like to defend their limiting beliefs because it feels "true" and relative, but the only way shit is going to change is by shifting your beliefs and altering the self-image to start experiencing a new reality.** The dominant image wins. Whatever you are thinking about self most, you are you going to attract, live, and experience. So would you rather attract your limiting beliefs, or more empowering beliefs?

That is all it is. I could go on and talk about how I have been neglected and rejected for multiple reasons in multiple ways. I could list out all that that I have accomplished, and how many others have had far greater opportunities having achieved far less. However, if I continue to think the way that I have always thought, I will continue to experience what I have always experienced So what is a more empowering belief or self-image? My time is coming. My time is coming, and I am being prepared. I am going to shake buildings. I am a Soul-mover and Spirit-awakener and my time is coming. I will continue to do the work because I love the process.

Truth is, I do not have to be on big stages to live my purpose anyway. I am here for the people. Whether it is on YouTube, in-person workshops, on the phone, or in a conversation, I am living my purpose every single day by helping people wake up to their inherent power. The form does not matter because I am living my dream. I am living my dream, and I will continue to attract opportunities when they are ready for me to receive. I am NOT going to continue the disempowering belief or self-image that I am going to be neglected or rejected because it is not bringing me the things I want in my life.

ΔΔΔ

ACTIVITY

When you envision your self-image, is there something right now that is holding you back from continuously attracting the things that you want? What disempowering beliefs do you have in your life? Why do you *choose* to continue to believe them? Would you rather suffer in your "truth" than experience the potential of a new reality? We change the world by changing ourselves. If we hold on to the negative self-limiting concepts, we continue to have to experience them until we have suffered enough that something has to change. Either way, change is inevitable. We can change by leaning into the pain of growth and evolution, or, we can suffer in the pain of staying the same until it becomes so fucking miserable that there is no other option. I am telling you right now, you do not have to wait. **Change the negative perception and end the suffering.**

DAY 39: GO DEEPER

SPECIAL CUEING TO OPTIMIZE YOUR BREATH HOLDS.

For the last four to five years I have been doing breath holds. Before that, I was performing 49 breaths, big diaphragmatic breathing with affirmations. Then I was introduced to holotropic breathwork, which is bigger, faster breathing for an extended period of time. It was not really until the end of my chiropractic student career (late 2013, early 2014) that I got introduced to the work of Wim Hof and that is when I started doing more breath holds. Eventually, I created my own breathing style, which I call Vortex Breathing. Hopefully, one of these days, I can showcase it for y'all. It is the most intense thing I have ever created in regards to a physiological and spiritual experience with breathing.

When performing breath holds, a lot of people will tell themselves to "hold longer" when feeling the burn to breathe again. What I have found to be a more effective cue is to tell yourself to "go deeper." **Going "longer" does not provide an adequate psychological**

reward for the endured pain associated with the stress of big breath holds. But, "deeper" crafts room for dimensional exploration, and that is something to get excited about.

When we shift our conscious awareness to consciousness itself, in the depths of a breath you can start to actually retract conscious thought, which in my physical experience is typically on the forehead or projecting from the forehead. As you deepen in the breath, you can deepen in the awareness, journeying inward into brain tissue, focusing on the pineal gland, and as you tell yourself to "go deeper," you will begin to experience altered states.

For me, I almost get into a full body vibrational shake where I start to see flashes or bursts of color which is also similar to visuals found in psychedelic experiences. Typically you will find that as you do more rounds of breath holds, your blood cells are more oxygenated. The more oxygenated your red blood cells are, the longer you can naturally hold your breath.

Wim Hof teaches 30 large diaphragmatic breaths. First, your belly expands, then your ribs, then your collarbone to fill the upper part of the lung space. It is a three-part breath all happening at one time. The breath is in and out of the mouth. Powerful inhale and relaxed exhale. On your 30th breath, you allow all your air out and hold the exhale for as long as you can. When you feel the need to breathe, hold that inhale for 10-seconds, then breathe normally. Remember, the cue is to tell yourself to "go deeper" when you feel the need to breathe. There are layers to this. There will be times when you think you need to breathe, but you can keep going, just enjoy the journey.

I love the breath hold because I can continually test to see the status of my system. I feel like I am training the ability to remain calm in seemingly sympathetic environments. When my nerve system is starting to feel anxiety from the need to breathe, I find my center, lower the vibration, and GO DEEPER.

Cues:

1. Go deeper vs hold longer

2. Having a count you are going for in the hold can help—remember it gets easier with more rounds

DAY 40: THE SACRED DANCE

THE PERSON WE ARE & THE PERSON WE ARE BECOMING. THE SACRED DANCE.

Last night I had a gathering of Kairos Training Culture facilitators from Life West Chiropractic College. One of the people brought up how they find themselves frustrated with where they are currently at with their skills and wanting to be better. That frustration was distracting them from being able to be present in service because they are always judging themself. This led to an empowering conversation and revelation.

When in service, you are exactly who you need to be in that moment. Whoever you have the opportunity to work with is exactly who needs you. That person chose you! God chose you! Know that exactly who you are now is enough and learn to be in gratitude, presence, love, patience, and peace—the biggest connectors to the now—working from the mind, to the Soul, to the Spirit. When we are connecting with people, we must love ourselves exactly the way we are, knowing that in the sacred dance between who we are and who we are becoming, the focus is on who we are now.

When training, we can shift our focus to being the criticizer and judger of where we are currently at and hold space for where we want to go. In training is when we can give ourselves the insights and open moments to notice what we notice. Yes, there is always going to be room to be better, but if you only live life thinking about where you want to be, you never live life in the now, and you are losing out on the power that you have in the moment.

There is always a version of us that will want more. That is not a bad thing, it is a great thing. But you have to be able to understand when to focus on one and when to focus on the other. In service, it is very very important that you are in the now, loving yourself now, knowing that who you are now is enough, and you can always transition into the other side of yourself that wants the growth.

When watching a chiropractic adjustment, many people focus on the impulse as being *the thing,* which I find very interesting. That would be like watching a dance performance and only looking at the spins or the jumps as *the thing.* If you have ever observed dance, especially between two people, when they come in and create suspense, and then pull away, you begin to realize the WHOLE performance is what makes it beautiful. Not just the big moments, also the space between the notes.

The adjustment actually happens from the inside. It happens from the adaptation from the communication of information. You can really consider the whole environment being part of the adjustment because as soon as they enter your space they are receiving information. They are receiving information by how they are greeted, by the energy of the space, by how they lay on the table, the music that is playing, the scents, the connection of the hands, the intention, the thoughts, the perceptions, all of it.

If you can understand how an entire experience is contributing to an adjustment, you can begin to understand how vital your thought process is along the way. If you are doubting your skill or ability, that lack of confidence is being communicated to the person you are serving, creating doubt and distrust within them. So, in the dance between connection and chase of perfection, you want to move with 100 percent certainty when it is service time.

I will tell you right now the one who is more certain wins. The one who is more connected to the ideal image wins. For all the people we get to interact with, if their image for themself is stronger than the image you have for them, and that image is very disempowering, the disempowering image wins. Healing is in the business of shifting perspectives and paradigms. **Healers are artists of ideal healing images.**

We need to be able to balance growth and connection. It is not an equal share all the time. You need to be able to swing the pendulum to love, gratitude, presence, and peace to who you are now so that you can have moments of being in 100 percent certainty, especially during times of service. Then you can swing the pendulum to growth so that you can get better with training. Honor this sacred dance.

ΔΔΔ

ACTIVATION

At this moment I allow myself to feel the
depths of who I am here, now
I feel an immense amount of gratitude
For all the work that has already been done
For all the training
For all the challenges I've already overcome
For exactly who I am now is enough
People that surround me benefit from who
I am here in this moment
For as much as I love the pursuit of the best version of myself that I can dream up
I love the connection to who I am now
At this moment I feel grateful
Grateful for all that I have

Grateful for the little things that people take for granted
Grateful for continuing to have an able body
To push, to move
Grateful to have lungs to breathe
Grateful for a strong heartbeat
And a warm bed to sleep in
Grateful for a roof over my head
Grateful for my family
Grateful for my relationships
Grated for my opportunities
I am grateful

DAY 41: DEEP QUESTIONS = DEEP AWARENESS

OUR PERCEPTION RESIDES AT THE DEPTH OF OUR AWARENESS.

The depth of our awareness is influenced by our relationship with Spirit and Soul and our openness and willingness to change (adaptability). Increased awareness and consciousness strengthens our vibrational broadcasting frequency, and with focus, it gives us more attractive, manifesting power. There is little else that is of more importance than continually expanded awareness.

How we currently perceive the world is based on our level of awareness. **The depths of our awareness will be dependent on the depths of our ques-**

tions. Most people blindly accept information without seeking further detail and understanding. It is important to ask questions that test the strength of the information being communicated. That's how we get better. That is how we evolve.

There is an amazing upside to this. There can be a downside as well. The downside is when you are consistently complicating things. Not everything needs to be complicated. However, you can develop a depth of understanding without complication. Complexity is an attribute of the ego. **The ego loves complexity. The Soul loves simplicity.**

How can you be questioning things all the time and also be moving into simplicity? There comes a point where you don't need to go wider, you just need to go deeper. The concept doesn't need to change, the depth of understanding changes. You can still be working with a similar concept of enlightenment—something exposing you to Universal truth—and you don't need to broaden that truth, you just need to deepen it. The questions aren't designed to complicate it but to give you more clarity. From clarity comes certainty, and our certainty increases with great questions as an ally.

My current definition of Love is, "a deepening of understanding of SELF." This is why I believe we will continue to feel love in relationships where we are discovering more of SELF. The number one thing I realize about Kate, and why she is a good strategy for love, is because she asks the questions that nobody else is asking. Her questions require me to be In-Spirit and access more of SELF.

As we continue to expand our awareness in consciousness, we strengthen our broadcasting vibrational frequency. It is like how myelin sheaths wrapping neural tissue can enhance the signal of nerve. Every time we deepen our awareness, we are becoming more effective beings of communication. If I have a depth of understanding of the concept of healing, then as I communicate or facilitate the healing process, I am carrying some potent medicine (knowledge and wisdom). And as we said before, the one who is more certain wins.

This is why I think Reggie Gold was so strong. He was one of the most incredible philosophers within chiropractic of all time. He had many debates with the medical profession. When you heard him speak, it was to a point where you felt that his level of clarity and certainty about the principles of life were so deeply understood that he was Unshakeable.

He was Unshakeable because nobody in the world could question him deeper than the level he questioned his own beliefs. We are easily shook when we superficially accept things as true and we do not do the work to investigate the depth of that understanding. Then when someone comes along and asks a simple question, and we have no answer because we have not explored it within our self, what tends to happen is we try to make that person wrong, or we want to fight or combat them in a different way.

This is why it is so crucial to STAY OPEN. Your openness, willingness to adapt to change, to evolve, and to be wrong, are some of the greatest strategies for continued evolution in consciousness. The second you close yourself off and become rigid in an idea, you become rigid in consciousness, and it becomes nearly impossible to expand. Expansion into the fourth dimension is what gives you the power to manifest and attract. What else is more important than that? What else is more important than your ability to create in this third-dimensional world? What else has more impact and influence?

Strategies:

1. Be open

2. Be willing to learn

3. Be willing to be wrong

4. Value adaptability

5. Question your level of understanding for depth

6. Remember you do not have to go wider, just go deeper

DAY 42: COMPARISON

FOCUS ON YOUR OWN NEEDS & PURPOSE.

I want to paint the current reality of what my day looked like yesterday. I want to do this because I know some people live their lives in comparison. I think it is essential to start to show what my life is really like, especially for those people who are inspired by me. Yesterday, I woke up at about 2:30 a.m. and began to write out some of the lessons and activations for a group I am leading. By 4:45 a.m., I started performing my daily movement, breathwork, and meditation in the sauna. Then I drop-in live on Facebook for the Unshakeables for 10 to 15 minutes. After that, I get prepared for the day to be at The Source Chiropractic by 6:45 a.m. to properly clear the space and get in the vibration of service.

One of my associates is currently in Puerto Rico, so on top of my full schedule, I am taking care of his people as well. We served patients non-stop from 7:15 a.m. to 12:30 p.m. Then, I met my wife for lunch where we are talking, still, about business and nanny coordination for our kids. Then, back to The Source at 2 p.m. to prep for service and finish reports. From 3-6:30 p.m. I'm serving patients again, non-stop, and from there at 7 p.m. I go live on Facebook for 45 minutes. After that, I have a meeting from 7:45-8:30 p.m., and another one until 9 p.m.. I finally get home around 9 and get a little bit of time to be Dad and put the kids to bed. Then around 10:30 p.m. I finally pass out. From 2:30 a.m. to 9:30 p.m. was my work day.

The reason I bring this up is that I do believe certain people look at my lifestyle or what you get to see—the success and achievement—and are inspired by it, but they do not understand what that day actually looks like. I don't know about you, but how many of you would choose that day? Would you choose to wake up at 2:30 a.m. and work straight for 19 hours? Is that your ideal life? At this moment, that is my reality, and I just want to be honest with you.

Fulfillment is about meeting *your* needs. For whatever reason, I have a purpose that pushes me to extremes at times. I believe it has a lot to do with all of the trauma that I have gone through in my life. I remember thinking that because my brother died young, I may die young. So every single day, I attempt to squeeze as much out of life as possible. When I die, I want the people at my memorial to say, "He gave everything he had, every single day. He died with no potential left."

I know that the way I live my life is that is not for everybody. So do not get lost in comparison cycles, because your life and how you choose to design it may look completely freaking different. And there is nothing wrong with that. This is about you. You may get to see people's highlight reels on social media, but you do not often get to see what they are doing minute by minute or hour to hour. I just wanted to illuminate what running five corporations can be like. I am not saying it is always like this, but when you are launching a business, good luck if you do not put in the work!

DAY 43: THE YIN WAY INTO THE HEART

DISCOVER THE POWER OF FEMININE SURRENDER.

Just had my fourth plant medicine journey and it has allowed me to open up in a brand new way. I feel like Source has been guiding me to dive deeper into my feminine and yin energy, and as I continue to deepen into this understanding, I realize how much more there is to learn. It just goes deeper and deeper.

I arrived at the property on Saturday, and the facilitators were very intentional about all that went into the ceremony. We started with a 1-hour meditation outside on a deck surrounded by mighty redwoods. After that, we did a breathwork session like I have never experienced. I feel like all of my major breakthroughs in entering altered states and evolving in consciousness have come from a very masculine or yang entry. Sure, enlightening has occurred during my meditations, but I feel like the majority of my meditative awakenings have traditionally been led first with a push in movement and breathwork.

The breathwork we did on Saturday is called Transformational Breathwork, and it was created in the 1970s by Dr. Judith Kravitz. It is an open-mouth style of breathwork that carries a feminine or yin energy. When I had performed breathwork in the past through the mouth, I would typically purse my lips and contort my body in an attempt to lead more air into my lungs. Right away, the primary facilitator came to my side and told me, “when you use your back to breathe, that is a very masculine force —a push.” She said, “just open your mouth, feel the air first enter the pelvic diaphragm, feel your belly expand, and then connect it to your heart.” For whatever reason, this was extremely difficult for me to do. Allowing air in, instead of forcing air in, was not only unfamiliar, but it also revealed a whole other layer of vulnerability within me. I realized I had been using the "control" of my breathing as a defense mechanism, and to relinquish the masculine energy of it felt like I was dropping my guard, exposing my essence and wounds of abandonment.

This breathwork session ended up being one of the most awakening sessions I have ever had. What I experienced in my body and in my consciousness was the power of feminine energy to heal and reveal new layers of SELF. My whole body was buzzing, and there was an energy pulsing throughout my system that I had never felt before. Every time I returned to my masculine habits of wanting to push, I would be pulled out of the Divine energy flow. As I continued to surrender, the energy would become vibrant and full.

The facilitators also taught something called "toning" during this breathwork session. When we were feeling energy build up, we were instructed to sound "ahhhhhhh" out loud and continue to connect and allow that energy to emerge. My body was going insane. It felt like the toning would find these energetic pockets within my system, expose them, and then vibrate them to join the Universal SELF. I became cavernous, as deep as the oceans.

As we moved from the breathwork and into the ceremony, the whole night was full of lessons of surrender. I began to discover that there are many dimensions that cannot be reached by the push, they need to be relaxed into. **To be whole, we need to honor the masculine AND the feminine.** This is where we find our full SELF.

DAY 44: EXCELLENCE IS ABOUT ALLOWING

EXCELLENCE IS LESS ABOUT WHAT YOU DO & MORE ABOUT WHAT YOU ALLOW.

Earlier this year when I was in Scottsdale, Arizona for Christmas, I was listening to a book called *Extreme Ownership* by Jocko Willink and Leif Babin, both former Navy Seals. One of the biggest concepts I grasped from this book came in this one line, "When it comes to performance standards, it's not what you preach, it's what you tolerate." What I took from this was when I look at the relationships and groups I belong in, if we are not expressing a level of excellence that I envision or would want, it is because subpar performance is being allowed or "tolerated."

This happens with all of us. Throughout the day, there will be things that get said that you just let slide. Or actions being performed that you do not agree with and they do not get addressed. However, when you do not address them, you are setting the guidelines for what is acceptable in your business or in your life. **I believe the biggest reason we do not address subpar behavior or performance is because we never took the time to get organized enough to even have standards!** Let's let that sink in for moment… If you do not have standards for your business, you do not have a business. If you do not have standards for your life, you are living someone else's.

When it comes to leadership, people will either rise to the level of your standards or fall to the level of their training. Either way, it is all on you. If you do not like what is happening around you, it is because YOU are allowing it. Standards are formed from repetitive behavior and organization. Lack of organization, especially for the ideators and creators, will leave you with no standard other than what is in your mind. It is extremely difficult for people to get in alignment with what is only in your mind. So, one must organize their thoughts. One must demonstrate repetitive behavior in action. From repetitive behavior, action, and organized thoughts, you can have standards. From your standards, you can hold the line. Otherwise, it will be near impossible to duplicate excellence.

Excellence is less about what you do, and more about what you allow. Understand the yin in that statement. When I first heard it, it felt authoritarian. Like it was about setting standards to follow and not accepting anything else. The yin perspective is: excellence is less about what you do (the masculine) and more about what you allow to emerge (the feminine). It's like when Michelangelo was asked how did you sculpt the Statue of David, he replied, "Simple, I just remove everything that is not David."

How do we realize and actualize our greatness? We remove everything that is not. In the depths of who we are is this infinite potential, wisdom, abundance, and power. Just start removing the shit that is not that. Discover the inner genius. Listen for the bigness. Listen for that which is constantly redirecting and causing adaptation and growth and evolution—for that is life. Remove what is not. Allow! It is less about what you do and more about what you allow. What are you allowing to emerge from within? Can you follow the deep inner voice of the God within? How do you keep the people in your life accountable? Do you have standards? If you don't have standards, it is time to get organized!

You cannot break the unbreakable. So how do we become Unshakeable? We become more connected to the depths of our purpose and the depths of our being. We stand in our truth, and our truth is Universal. We remove what is not, and step into what is and what has always been. For NOW is our time.

DAY 45: YIN MEDITATION

GUIDED BREATHING & MEDITATION FOR THOSE OF US THAT ARE NEEDING TO BE.

It is easy to get lost in the DOING. At this point, some of you may be thinking I have multiple personalities. It is because I do. We all do. Because **we are not what we do, we are who we are.** We are large, we contain multitudes. It is important to find balance and rhythm in the dynamism of our nature. It is important to be able to flow between the masculine and the feminine, and anything in between, knowing that by being Divine we are a representation of ALL.

ΔΔΔ

ACTIVITY

Breathwork & Meditation

This is a gentle yin way into the heart space for transformation. It is a tool or asset to be used when you are feeling like a lot of your action has become masculine in nature, and a lot of your awareness is being forced, and you require the feminine recuperative energy. Notice how the breathing and thought process shifts. Notice how the inner dialogue transforms.

Find your ears over your shoulders and your
shoulders over your hips
We are going to do some nasal breathing, and I want
you to focus on little to no back movement
As you inhale just let the belly expand and come forward
Now that air needs to come up the chest, and you
want to anchor it into your heart space
Do not assist that breath with an arch of your back
Try to keep your back in a neutral position
And inhale for seven seconds, belly expands, keep inhaling
Little to no back movement, but feel it in your heart
When you catch it in your heart, hold for three seconds
Then exhale through the nose for seven
Hold for three
Inhale through the nose for seven
Feel the buzz in the heart, hold for three
Exhale through the nose, hold
Inhale, belly expands, no movement from the back

Continue that, and hold
Exhale..... Hold
Inhale ..... Hold
Exhale
You are going to continue this breathing pattern as I talk
Long seven count, belly expands
Allowing that energy to rise into the heart
with no back movement
Feel the tingle in the heart, feel that awareness
in the heart space, allow it to enter
Hold for three count, exhale for long seven
count, hold for three count
As you go through this process feel the air just
being allowed to enter and to exit
You don't have to force anything
It just moves through you
Continue to allow it to happen
As you continue this breathing, your heart will gain
more and more awareness and sensation
Continue to breathe into it
Imagine that the heart is encased in cement
As you first start breathing you are no-
ticing the harder outer layer
And you just notice what you notice

No judgment of why it chooses to be like that
With every breath, a little more of it crumbles away
Being able to sense with your awareness, the softening, with every breath, a little softer
A little less rigid
Continuing to breathe until you reach the sacred heart space outer layer
Imagining giving the heart a warm hug
You get to feel the softness of your heart
you feel the warmth, you feel the light
As you embrace the light, that warmth becomes magnified
Your chest opens, just a little bit more
A little smile comes upon your face
Knowing that you can be fully seen by Self
That you can be fully heard by Self
You can be fully felt by Self
In that embrace with the heart, you see all of you
All of who you are now
All of what you have been through
With unconditional love and compassion, you hold yourself
Continue to breathe
Feel all you feel
Know that you are enough

Know that you are where you are supposed to be
Know that everything you need is right here

DAY 46: SAVOR THE SLOWDOWN

MAXIMIZE YOUR RECOVERY & MATCH TONE WITH THE UNIVERSAL "SLOWDOWN."

This lesson comes from many years of push. I am learning more and more to appreciate the moments of the "slowdown." This lesson is great for many of us that carry energy that likes to move and produce. What I have become more sensitive to is understanding cycles, seasons, and universal vibrations. In my office, this last week has been uncharacteristically slow. We are noticing more cancellations and reschedules, less new people, and It seems like there are fewer practice visits as well.

This is my fifth year in practice, and this type of slowdown is much different than the other kinds of slowdowns I have experienced before. This is a Universal slowdown. This is why I mentioned earlier that **there is nothing I can think of that is more important than continually increasing your awareness**. What I am feeling right now in regards to our practice slowdown is that the Universe is asking us to reorganize for a new area of growth. What often happens, is when things slow down, people get frustrated. They feel something must be wrong. If you have the appropriate awareness, you will be able to differentiate between when there is something actually wrong with the business, and when Universe is giving you signs that you need recuperation or reorganization.

If you continue to try and push when Universe is trying to give you a recovery period, you will miss your opportunity for Spiritual growth. The reason for the slowdown is for you to get organized and work on the foundation. It is to make sure that everything is optimized in a way that when the growth period comes again, you are ready and can be bigger, better, more efficient, and more stable than you were before.

If you do not notice the Universal slowdown indicator and you get frustrated and try to push because you feel like something is wrong, then your system never got the opportunity to receive what it really needed. There will be times for growth, expansion, and push. There will also be times for recovery, reorganization, and the pull. It is a beautiful thing to be able to sense this and communicate it with your team. Learn to appreciate and savor the slowdowns. These times are rare. Savor it. Find that space. Recover. And do not worry, the next expansion is on its way.

ΔΔΔ

ACTIVATION

I am
We are not our titles
We are
When you realize the depth of the "I Am"
you realize it is the ALL
The big SELF
In this moment I am grateful
For my continued awareness
And the expansion of that awareness
And the expansion of consciousness
Knowing that as my consciousness evolves
I find relationship in all things
I find relationship with all things
I will slow down when I need to slow down
And I will pick up when I need to pick up
Because I am ready!
I am ready to do the work
I realize that I am here to effort
And that the effort can come in ebbs and flows

Recovery periods allow me to reorganize
To restructure
So that when it comes time
Time for the push
Time for growth
I am ready to step into a new being
Not the old version of myself
But the new version
The 2.0, 3.0, 4.0
Wherever we are, we are better every single day
So I honor these moments
I savor the slowdown
I connect to my family
I connect to my friends
I listen
And I stay ready
My time is coming!

DAY 47: SHAMANISTIC EXPERIENCE VS RELIGION

DIRECT & INDIRECT PATHS TO GOD.

I began reading a book called *The Toltec Oracle.* It includes a deck of cards to be used as divination tools. The first 30 pages talk about the origin of the Toltecs, who date back further than the Aztecs or the Mayans. *The Four Agreements* written by Don Miguel Ruiz is also a book based on Toltec wisdom. I have been learning a lot about this wonderful philosophy. The Toltecs noticed everything manifested in this world from a dualistic view with two opposing sides *interacting* with one another. Typically, when people talk about dualism, they create separation and a battle between the two opposing sides. The Toltecs believed the key to life is the UNION of the two opposing sides. For example, one of the most prominent symbols within Toltec wisdom is the Quetzalcoatl - the "feathered serpent" (a serpent with eagle feathers). The serpent and eagle could easily be enemies, but if they unite they possess the power to awaken humanity.

One of my biggest revelations from *The Toltec Oracle* came from a chapter on Shamanism and the Shamanistic experience. When talking about the Shaman, Toltecs would say that **the Shaman FACILITATES an environment where you communicate with God, where you experience the divine.** The Shamanistic experience is your union with or direct experience of God. Whereas in religion, there is usually an intermediary. Whether it is the preacher, the gospel, the Bible, or saint or bishop, *they* are the ones trusted to communicate with God for you and you are supposed to follow their guidance. I am not saying either is good or bad, I am just sharing what is in this text.

Religion tends to require more faith, a fellowship, and a trust of what is being communicated. The Shamanistic experience requires a different kind of faith and bravery. The Shaman is not an intermediary with you and God. The Shaman is someone who has acquired spiritual knowledge and wisdom and facilitates experiences where YOU connect directly with God. Shamans empower you in your spiritual journey to learn sacred practices that help you develop a direct relationship with Source.

I find it interesting that Western culture projects so much weird shit onto Shamanistic ritual, Shamanistic experiences, and Shamans in general. A Shaman merely is someone who crafts an environment that allows you to experience God, and that is it. Julia Cameron is a master teacher of creativity. When people ask her how she can possibly teach someone to be creative, she replies "I don't, I craft the space that allows creativity to emerge." That's what a Shaman is doing. Cultivating space for Spiritual experiences to emerge.

When sharing what I was learning about Shamanism with Kate, she started laughing at me and said, "That's why I've been calling you the Urban Shaman!" In retrospect, yes, a lot of what I have been facilitating through various workshops and healing experiences is allowing people to connect to their Spirit SELF. Performing various forms of breathwork, meditation, and visualization to reach altered states of consciousness ARE forms of Shamanistic rituals. It is time to lose the "taboo" perspective on Shamanistic experiences and embrace our ability to directly connect with the Divine.

ΔΔΔ

ACTIVATION

I am exactly where I need to be

I am becoming all that I am supposed to be

I am present

I am connected
I am love
I am abundant
I take decisive action
I honor my values
I honor my vision
I honor the Intelligence
I am ready for the day
For all the challenges and for all the blessings
Knowing that it is a gift to receive both
Aho!

DAY 48: EFFORTING, IT'S WHY YOU'RE HERE

WE ARE HERE TO RECEIVE AS A RESULT OF EFFORT & TO GIVE LIKE GOD.

Yesterday a student from Life West came into The Source, and I could tell something was up. As I check-in with him, he says, "Yeah, I don't know what's wrong... something is really going on." I tell him to lay down so we can get him adjusted. When he gets up, I tell him he looks better, and continue to ask what was going on with him. He looked me straight in the eye and said, "I just don't want to jump through these mother-fucking hoops anymore." I looked him back in the eye and said, "that is exactly what you are here for."

It sounds silly, but it is true. Wherever you are, there will be challenges. Sometimes, they are not your preferred challenges (like trying to get through a graduate program). I get it. AND, I was recently reminded by my mentor Dr. Marvin Talsky that there are two reasons why we are here having a human experience. One is to experience what it feels like to give like God. Why? An ALL-powerful, ALL-present, and ALL-knowing Intelligence cannot experience what it feels like to give to another. As the infinite Source of Intelligence, there is no other, this is the principle of a non-dualistic reality.

The second reason we are here is to receive only as the result of effort. If you are efforting, that is a good thing! Even though it may not feel like it at times, it is a great thing to be efforting. That is what we came here for. Why? Because as God, as the Infinite ALL-knowing, ALL-present, and ALL-powerful Source, things happen for you in a snap. All reality is existing at all times, in all dimensions. As soon as you can think of it, there it is. There is no effort. **We are here having this human experience to feel and experience what it feels like to give like God and to receive only as a result of effort.** Pretty genius.

So, efforting is WHY we are here! Just laugh about it because you are going to have to effort, in one way or another, for the rest of your life. Consider it a blessing. If you are feeling tired, know there is another wave of energy coming. Remember, when connected to Soul and Spirit, the recuperation you need will be delivered within Divine timing. Everything that occurs in nature occurs in cycles, and you are part of nature! You are part of the Universe, and when you need to call on Source, when you need to call on

Spirit, it will be there, always, to guide you, to serve you, and to provide for you. So get out of your head, get into your heart, and effort.

DAY 49: YOU'VE GOT TO WANT THIS

YOU GOT TO WANT THIS SHIT! WANT TO BE HERE!

When I woke up this morning, there were a lot of things weighing on me, and I was feeling the pressure of stress caving in. Then suddenly, something switched and deep from my mind I heard the phrase, "I want this shit." Kevin Hart has a saying before he goes on stage, "Everybody wants to be famous, but nobody wants to do the work." My high school football coaches taught us to put four fingers in the air when it was the fourth quarter. This was a reminder to us all that it is in the fourth quarter that champions are made. See, in the first half of the game, when you are fresh and have energy, it's easy to play all-out. But in the fourth quarter, when you are tired and busted up, that's when the game is won.

The truth is, sometimes you will wake up, and just want to give up. There has to be something deep down inside of you—and there is—that allows you to flip the switch, to stand up in the sludge of discomfort and say, "I want this shit. This day matters, this moment matters, and that which I have dedicated myself to matters. I am willing to go through whatever it takes because I matter! I give a shit, and I want this shit!"

For those of you that need to hear it, know that we all have a built-in perseverance muscle. Sure, there will be cycles and seasons where you will recuperate. And, there will also be cycles and seasons where you feel like you need to recuperate, but you really need to fucking push on. Get your ass up, get moving, get talking, and play some hip-hop because it's GO time.

We are Unshakeable. Why? Because we are connected to something bigger than the small self. As we deepen this connection, we will discover new energetic reservoirs. We all have it. **We all have more than we think we do. Allow yourself to experience what "more" is by breaking through what has always been.**

DAY 50: SOULAR POWER

"THAT SOMETHING ELSE" WHEN IN ALIGNMENT WITH YOUR SOUL PURPOSE.

There are many different energies that we can interact with and utilize as a human being. One is our "life vitality" that is dependent upon our strategies of health and laws of the body. These laws include movement, nourishment, recuperation, recreation, and our mindset or mental energy. Honoring or neglecting these laws will increase or decrease our vitality on a day to day basis. There is also another energy that exists outside of life vitality, one I like to call SOULar energy. I believe this is an energy that becomes available when you are connected to your Soul's purpose.

As a refresher, we have the egoic mind, that which creates separation and what gives you an individual experience. You could also relate this to the educated mind. That which stores what you have learned in this lifetime. We also have the Soul. Soul energy engulfs physical matter and form. Soul has lived many lives, not necessarily in direct relationship with your ancestral lineage. We have the ancestors along our bloodline, and we also have our ancestors along our Soulline. **Our Soul has incarnated in multiple forms, in multiple time periods, and potentially even in multiple dimensions.**

Carrying "you" is a Soul that has existed since existence. Every Soul has a purpose. You could also consider it a Guide. The Soul is constantly trying to communicate with you, but are you listening? And are you aware enough and awake enough to receive the messages properly? We all know about the mental chatter—the voices that are everywhere and don't quit—but how many of us take the time to get quiet and hear the indicators of the Soul? Once you start to learn Soul's voice and how it communicates to you, you will have Soul guidance.

When operating in Soul guidance with Soul purpose you can be granted SOULar power. This is an extra resource that many don't tap into. Your physical body might be reaching a point where it is tired, and then BOOM - something else kicks in. If you are not connected to Soul purpose, but you are connected to the perceived purpose of your Ego, you will enter physical exhaustion and drain your life force. When you lose life force, you lose years off your life. So, know thy Soul, connect to SOULar Power, and ADD LIFE to your years!

DAY 51: THE POWER OF OUR FIELD

THE POWER OF OUR FIELD. ONCE WE CHANGE, EVERYTHING CHANGES. UNLESS WE EXPECT IT NOT TO.

There are layers of depth to today's message. Let's begin with a story from when I had a profound experience on my first journey with the "Grandmother." It was 2018, from December 31st to January 1st under a full moon. It was absolutely incredible. The work that happened that night was massive. It was thick and intense. Shit, it was a lot of things. The medicine delivered a lot of imagery about how I was showing up in life—especially as a parent, in relation to my boy.

Jax had a really rough time from birth to about three years old. He had difficulty with transitions and a lot of sensory issues. When he was having meltdowns, freakouts, and tantrums, we typically had a "need" to be somewhere. In those transitions, since I was "strong," I would do my best to gently carry him even though he was kicking, screaming, crying, and biting—I cannot tell you how many times I have been bitten by my own child—but I do not blame him, he was freaking out.

In my journey, I got to see the world from his perspective—he was feeling overwhelmed and unsafe, and then basically being man-handled against his will. That changed everything for me. The way we handle transitions with respect and reverence for my boy and his process is entirely different now. A lot changed for me within ten hours. When I came back home, my consciousness and awareness had shifted, and things were just different. I had not implemented any behavioral changes within myself yet, but there was already a change in my boy.

This is what I mean by the power of our field. This is very important. **As we awaken in awareness and consciousness, if everything shifts for us internally, then it also shifts for us externally, unless we expect it not to.** What often happens is we have an awakening, we obtain new insight, intuition, and guidance, yet we expect the people around us to behave the same. That is the mistake.

If it shifts for you, it shifts for everybody because we are a representation of the whole. The only way it does not shift for everybody is when you expect the same thing from them, and then your expectation literally re-creates the same behavior for them. If you move forward as if it has already changed and in an intention that it has changed for them too, watch what happens in your life and in your relationships. Watch how fast and quickly things have the ability to heal. Change does not have to be linear. There can be quantum healing in awakening and in relationships. It can happen for all, instantaneously, and it does.

DAY 52: KNOW WHO THE FUCK YOU ARE

YOU ARE THE UNIVERSE UNFOLDING AND EXPERIENCING ITSELF.

The time has come. We started off this journey with a talk about legacy. The opportunity was to envision how you wanted to be remembered. If you died today, what would people say about you? Would you like what you hear? If not, luckily there is still time, right?

At a recent event, those of us speaking were asked to write what we would say if we had to fit all of our wisdom onto one page. Here is what I wrote up:

You are the Universe unfolding and experiencing itself.

The being is limited when rigid and closed off from Source.

The being is unlimited when open and connected to Source.

For those wanting to experience a continual evolution in consciousness, awareness, and SELF-development, stay open and train your mind-body to connect to Source EVERY DAY.

The best time to start training connecting to Source is NOW.

The best type of training for connecting to Source is a sequence of movement - breath-work - meditation (in that order).

You will know you are successful when you begin to enter altered states of consciousness.

Altered states of consciousness are the pre-requisite for spiritual experiences.

Spiritual experiences expand our consciousness to receive insight from the unknown Infinite Vortex of wisdom.

It's in the Vortex that you will discover ALL.

If I'm gone in this physical realm, know that you can always join me in the Vortex.

For me, it is about *Knowing Who The Fuck You Are*. You are the Universe unfolding and experiencing itself. When open and connected to this Source of Intelligence you continue to evolve. You continue to experience love. Your perception in all relationships surrounding your life will be increased. You will have the option to choose a response instead of constantly react. When rigid and closed from Source, you will start to feel dis-ease. You will experience suffering because you will be living a life of misperception.

I can think of little else that is of more importance than to continually expand your awareness and evolve in consciousness. The top ways I know how to do that are movement, breathwork, and meditation, and in that order. If I am ever gone, enter an altered state of consciousness, enjoy a spiritual experience, and I'll meet you in the Vortex.